This book is given

in honor of
Jennifer Hart
By
Gordon & Eileen Hart
May 2000

Project Zero Frameworks for Early Childhood Education
Volume 1

Building on Children's Strengths:

The Experience of Project Spectrum

Project Zero Frameworks for Early Childhood Education
Volume 1

Howard Gardner
David Henry Feldman
Mara Krechevsky
General Editors

Building on Children's Strengths:
The Experience of Project Spectrum

Jie-Qi Chen
Mara Krechevsky
Julie Viens
with **Emily Isberg**

Teachers College · Columbia University
New York and London

Published by Teachers College Press, 1234 Amsterdam Avenue, New York, NY   10027

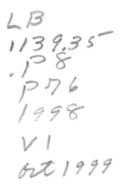

ISBN 0-8077-3766-6 (paper)
ISBN 0-8077-3817-4 (cloth)

Printed on acid-free paper

Manufactured in the United States of America
05   04   03   02   01   00   99   98   8   7   6   5   4   3   2   1

This book is for Daria, Harley, and Sophie

CONTENTS

ACKNOWLEDGMENTS

The work reported in this book would not have been possible without the generous funding of the William T. Grant Foundation, the Rockefeller Brothers Fund, the Spencer Foundation, and the National Institute of Child Health and Human Development. We are grateful to these organizations for their support.

Many individuals participated in guiding Spectrum through its different phases. First, and most important, we would like to extend our heartfelt thanks and appreciation to the parents and children who participated in our research at various sites in the Boston, Massachusetts, area: the Eliot-Pearson Children's School in Medford; the Cummings School, the Kennedy School, and the Winter Hill School in Somerville; the SMILE program, also in Somerville; and the Mason School in Roxbury. These families inspired us with their passion for learning and enthusiasm for exploring new educational terrain.

For their helping to smooth the rocky path from theory to practice during the first phase of research, we would like to thank the directors, teachers, and graduate students at the Eliot-Pearson Children's School: Betty Allen, Ellen Band, Jinny Chalmers, Carolee Fucigna, Matthew Goodman, Penny Hauser-Cram, Cynthia Lawrence, Priscilla Little, Sunita Mookerjee, Mark Ogonowski, and Ann Olcott; the members of the original research team who helped develop the assessment approach and activities: Margaret Adams, Jenifer Goldman, Lori Grace, Thomas Hatch, Laurie Leibowitz, Ulla Malkus, Valerie Ramos-Ford, Janet Stork, and Carey Wexler-Sherman; and the project consultants who contributed their wisdom and expertise: David Alexander, Kathy Cannon, Lyle Davidson, Martha Davis, Deborah Hicks, Matthew Hodges, Sylvia Feinburg, Lynn Meltzer, Larry Scripp, Joseph Walters, Ellen Winner, and Dennis Palmer Wolf. Thanks also go to Mindy Kornhaber and Janet Stork for helpful comments during the preparation of this book.

For their work on the Somerville project, we would like to thank the public school teachers, Mary Ann DeAngelis, Pamela Holmes, Marie

Kropiwnicki, and Jean McDonagh, who implemented the Spectrum activities in their classrooms and gave us valuable feedback; former superintendent of schools John Davis and Director of Curriculum Wayne LaGue, who supported Spectrum research in their district; project researchers Roger Dempsey, Corinne Greene, Miriam Raider-Roth, and Winifred O'Toole for their work in developing Spectrum activities and collaborating with teachers; and our research assistants, Andrea Bosch, Jill Christiansen, Jim Gray, Elise Miller, and Ilyse Robbins Mohr, who helped observe the implementation of Spectrum activities in the classroom. Thanks also to the project consultants, Ann Benjamin, Lyn Fosoli, and Roger Weissberg, for their useful comments and suggestions.

For their participation in our collaboration with the Boston Children's Museum and the Somerville SMILE program, we are grateful to all our museum partners, especially the museum interpreters. Special thanks go to Jeri Robinson and Jane Moore for heading up the museum team, and to Cheryl Seabrook-Wilson for graciously sharing her SMILE classroom with us. We are grateful also to our colleagues on the research team, Rochelle Frei and project manager Valerie Ramos-Ford, for their insights and hard work.

On the Spectrum Connections Project, we owe a very special thanks to our mentors Leo Boucher, Jackie Cooper, Aldo Ghirin, Vineet Gupta, Amatul Hannan, Reginald Jackson, John Piasta, Ron Reid, Reggie Sampson, and Lena Saunders, who brought friendship, skill, and passion to their weekly visits with the children. We worked with a superb and dedicated research team: Amy Norton, Nathan Finch, and Miriam Raider-Roth; Heping Hao helped with data analysis. We are indebted also to Mason School teachers Mary O'Brien, Gwen Stith, and Lindsay Trementozzi, principal Mary Russo, and Parent Advisory Council members Susan Donath, William Moran, and Debbie Rambo for their inspired contributions and commitment to the program; and to the staff and consultants with Boston Partners in Education, Lonnie Carton, Marta Dennis, and Arthur Kempton, who lent their expertise at critical junctures in the project.

For the description of Spectrum work in the field, we are indebted to William Bruns, Karen Bulman, Bruce Campbell, Sheila Callahan-Young, Julie Carter, Margaret Daugherty, Patricia Fernandes, Jo Gusman, Carol Hylton, Christa Norment, Hilda Rosselli, Joyce Rubin, Pam Prue, and Wave Starnes, who shared with us valuable information regarding their beliefs, insights, and experiences in applying MI theory to their educational practices. We would like to thank Mindy Kornhaber for sharing with us school observation notes and insights gained through her doctoral research.

Our sincerest thanks also go to Emily Isberg, for her editorial expertise and for helping to blend our diverse voices into a coherent story; to Brian Ellerbeck of Teachers College Press, for his wise counsel and patience in guiding this book to publication; and to Lori Tate, also of Teachers College Press, for turning our words into print.

PREFACE

In this book we present the history of Project Spectrum, a 10-year research project dedicated to developing an alternative approach to curriculum and assessment—one that respects the diverse interests and abilities that children bring to the preschool and early elementary classroom.

In the following pages, we describe what happened when a set of psychological theories moved from their creators' minds, into the classroom, and some time later, out into the community at large. These theories, Howard Gardner's theory of multiple intelligences (MI theory) and David Henry Feldman's nonuniversal theory, present a powerful vision of the different ways that individuals learn. When applied to early childhood education, these ideas suggest that each child exhibits a distinctive profile of different abilities, or multiple intelligences; moreover, rather than being fixed, these intelligences can be enhanced by an educational environment rich in stimulating materials and activities.

Through Spectrum classrooms, we tried to find out how our convictions could best be put into practice. Through this book, we hope to share with our readers—professional educators and others who care passionately about the schooling of our nation's children—the insights we gained as our investigation developed in unexpected ways.

Building on Children's Strengths is a team effort, written collaboratively by five of the many researchers who contributed to Spectrum over the years: David Henry Feldman of Tufts University and Howard Gardner of Harvard University's Project Zero, who founded the project and provided its theoretical framework; Mara Krechevsky, who directed the effort to assess strengths in young children; Jie-Qi Chen, who was interested in building on strengths to help children who were struggling with basic skills; and Julie Viens, who worked on bringing community resources into the classroom. Freelancer Emily Isberg joined us to help write and edit the book. Together, we planned and executed the narrative portion; Krechevsky, Chen, and Viens contributed equally, hence the alphabetical order of the author names. An individually authored introduction and conclusion frames the book: In these two chapters, David Henry Feldman and Howard Gardner, respectively, reflect upon the project's goals and accomplishments.

In the first chapter, Feldman presents Spectrum's theoretical roots—his nonuniversal theory and Gardner's MI theory—against the backdrop of more-traditional views of human intelligence. The two theories provide convincing arguments that children have a far wider range of abilities than generally are valued in school or measured by IQ and other standardized tests. Many students who have been labeled deficient on the basis of pencil-and-paper tests may have strengths in the visual arts, movement, social understanding, or other areas that could be used as entry points into the school curriculum.

In Chapter 2, we describe our work in a Medford, Massachusetts, preschool to develop assessments that would paint a broad but detailed picture of childrens' strengths. Through our experience in the classroom, we found that very often we could not assess children without providing some sort of instruction first. As we tried to evaluate children in the context of performing real-world tasks, we asked them to use the "tools of the trade"—paints or markers for visual arts, pliers for mechanical science, toy figures for the storytelling components of language. Sometimes the children were unfamiliar with the materials or the way that the materials had to be used to perform the task. So we spent time developing activities to introduce children to the types of abilities we wished to assess. As a result, we created a classroom environment where assessment and curriculum were designed to constantly reinforce each other, both promoting and examining children's accomplishments in a field.

In Chapter 3, we present the second phase of the project, during which we explored whether the academic performance of at-risk children could be improved by discovering and fostering their areas of strength. We examine the difficulties that teachers encountered as they set up learning centers where children could explore musical instruments, carpentry tools, and other stimulating materials, and the excitement they felt upon discovering abilities in their students they had not imagined before. We look at the techniques they devised to use these children's abilities and interests as pathways into the academic curriculum.

The next two chapters explore our attempts to link the classroom with the vast educational resources of the community as a way of developing children's strengths more fully. In particular, we turned to children's museums, where children can learn by pursuing their own interests at their own pace; and to mentors, a group of artists, athletes, city planners and other professionals who were matched, on the basis of their strengths and interests, with students in one of Boston's most economically deprived neighborhoods. In Chapter 4 we present what we found out about integrating learning experiences in a children's museum with those in the classroom. In Chapter 5 we describe what happened when we invited mentors into the classroom to help teach.

Project Spectrum, as a formal research project, ended in 1993. But the ideas it generated have taken on a life of their own. Schools and communities around the country have adopted what they liked best about the Spectrum approach, using it to revamp curriculum, develop performance-based assessments, expand the definition of "gifted and talented," integrate special needs students into the classroom, communicate with children who don't speak English, and create a schoolwide culture where teachers work together toward a common goal. In Chapter 6, we take a look at four situations in which educators have, in their own unique ways, used a Spectrum approach to address problems they wished to correct. Through these stories, involving public elementary schools outside of Boston, New York City, Washington, DC, and Seattle, we try to identify the qualities that characterize a "Spectrum classroom" or school.

In Chapter 7, Gardner looks back on the many different ways that his and Feldman's theories have shaped classroom practice, and that classroom experience has, in turn, informed their ideas about cognitive development. In many ways, he explains, Spectrum has served as a bridge: between theory and practice, teacher and researcher, school and community, and perhaps most important, a child's area of strength and the required curricular skills.

Spectrum is not a set of tests or curricular units. Instead, it is a framework, a way of thinking about children's growth and children's strengths. We hope it provides some new ideas, inspiration, and support for your efforts to create an optimal educational atmosphere for the children in your care.

CHAPTER 1

How Spectrum Began

David Henry Feldman

Suppose a child has the potential for astonishing grace and expressiveness in movement, but her teachers steadfastly avoid all movement activities because of their own inhibitions and negative childhood experiences. Suppose another child loves and is capable of expressing himself through music, but neither his teachers nor his parents listen to music, play an instrument, or sing with him. Suppose another child thinks in pictures, clearly envisioning a map, or a timeline, or the way in which the parts of a pencil sharpener are put together, but her teachers consider her slow because she can't express her ideas in words.

What happens to these children? Do they muddle along, struggling with curricula that might be clear if presented in a different way? Do they appear somewhat deficient by traditional school standards, only to show off their talents later as inventors, singers, airplane pilots, machinists, tennis instructors, piano tuners, engineers? Or are they labeled a failure so often that they simply give up trying? What is lost when a child's potential has no outlet for expression? What could be gained by trying to recognize the unique contributions each child can make?

Today, in the face of widespread concern about the quality of public education, we are faced with a dizzying number of proposals for school reform. Suggested changes range from relatively modest ones, such as instituting new rules for teacher certification, to radical ones, such as turning the system over to the private sector. Others include greater choice for families regarding which schools their children will attend, or the redistribution and equalizing of increasingly scarce resources. One that is particularly troublesome, however, is a call for standardizing the curriculum, focusing rigidly on the basic skills required to function in today's society.

The issue is not the importance of the basic curriculum. Certainly reading, arithmetic, and the like are essential goals of schooling. Our point is different: there are many paths toward productive and worthwhile participation in society. It should be equally as important to our schools and families to discover what each child can uniquely contribute as it is to make sure that each child has the skills to function well in society.

Furthermore, we object to the idea that all children should be expected to learn the same things in the same way. A growing body of evidence (H. Gardner, 1983, 1993; Sternberg, 1985) shows that human minds are not all the same. There are many different ways of knowing and thinking about the world. Thus, the more teachers and schools know about their students and the different ways that they learn, the more teachers and schools can help them acquire the skills they value most.

For those who wish to make schools more uniform, attending to children's individual differences may be a luxury we can ill afford. But in our eyes, acknowledging this diversity is both a necessity and a powerful lens for focusing efforts at school reform. If we overlook the broad range of human abilities to concentrate on those few that show up on paper-and-pencil tests, we are dooming many children to years of frustration and disappointment, if not outright failure. By contrast, we believe that it is possible to employ an array of human interests and abilities—in domains such as music, visual arts, movement, social concern—toward the goal of helping all our children learn at their best.

A decade ago, Howard Gardner and I, supported by a collaborative research group from Harvard University's Project Zero and Tufts University, first launched Project Spectrum—an effort to identify distinctive intellectual strengths in young children. We decided to start at the preschool level. In part, we wanted to find out just how early the various intellectual potentials could be detected. But we also believed that the sooner children's strengths were identified, the more time children, teachers, administrators, and parents would have to work together to develop them, and the less time there would be for children with strengths in nontraditional areas to fall through the cracks. Several studies have shown that, as early as the third grade, one can use measures of academic performance to predict those students who will drop out before completing high school (cf. Slavin, Karweit, & Madden, 1989). Although there are many ways to interpret these studies, it appears that if school has not engaged a child during the first few years, the chance may be lost forever.

We launched Project Spectrum with a grant from the Spencer Foundation in 1984. At the time, we were deeply involved, in our own separate ways, in exploring the nature of human cognition. Several years earlier, I had published the book *Beyond Universals in Cognitive Development* (1980/1994), examining the many realms of development beyond those common to all children. Howard Gardner had just published *Frames of Mind* (1983/

1993), in which he advanced the now well-known theory of multiple in-telligences (MI theory), an attempt to broaden the definition of human thought. Although our work had begun as scientific inquiry, the public response awakened us to its profound educational implications. We were eager to see if we could develop methods of assessment more faithful to the broad scope of human intellectual endeavor than prevailing measures, in large part standardized tests.

We selected the project name to represent the broad array, or spec-trum, of intelligences, styles, and proclivities that we expected each child to present. We hoped to raise the consciousness of teachers, parents, and the children themselves to the many possibilities for productive expres-sion of potential that a wider view of abilities might bring. The trick, of course, was finding ways to assess the diversity we believed was there.

Although it took considerable effort and more time than we expected, we found through Spectrum that it is indeed possible to use alternative methods to assess strengths in children as young as 4 years old. We then explored ways in which classroom teachers and curriculum planners could use this information to better tailor instructional, curricular, and class-room design to individual needs, and to reflect upon their own experience and practice (Schön, 1983).

After this, we were ready to test our assessment activities in an urban elementary classroom. We used information about children's strengths to develop interventions for first-grade children at risk for school failure. Because few teachers have expertise in all the learning areas where chil-dren might excel, we next tried to link the school with community re-sources. We developed a collaboration between a preschool and a chil-dren's museum, and matched first graders with mentors who had similar strengths and interests. Even after the project formally drew to a close, the ideas continued to evolve. Educators around the country took up the banner, adapting the Spectrum approach to their own particular needs.

Each time we tried to extend the reach of Spectrum into new areas, we found challenges, questions, and constraints that were often unantici-pated and that required adaptations in our techniques. Over the years, we became more aware of how difficult it will be to solve some of the prob-lems in education, how interconnected are both the sources and resistance to change, and how each new situation must be understood and appreci-ated for what it can teach us about human diversity. Yet we tried through-out to retain the project's central aims: to find ways to enhance the early experience of young children by identifying their distinctive strengths, giving support to these strengths, and helping teachers, parents, and the children themselves celebrate their diverse potentials.

CONTRASTING VIEWS OF ASSESSMENT

Although there are many educators who share our desire for alternative methods of assessment (see Meisels, 1989) at times we feel as if we are trying to push back a tide—a tide of public opinion set in motion by the 1983 publication of *A Nation at Risk* (D. Gardner, 1983). In this highly publicized and influential document, a national commission reached the conclusion that public education in this country was inferior to that of other countries and losing ground. In large part, it made its case with results from the Scholastics Aptitude Test (SAT) and various internationally oriented comparative paper-and-pencil instruments.

These condemnations gave new ammunition to the "back-to-basics" movement, a response to a perceived relaxing of standards, diluting of the public school curriculum, and retreat from traditional practice with respect to such matters as discipline, authority, and teacher preparation. One solution, recently endorsed by President Clinton, is the establishment of national academic standards, with student achievement monitored through increased use of standardized tests. Once again, we must state that we have no objection to academic rigor, or the setting of standards. Indeed, in the process of setting standards, teachers, administrators, parents, and all the other members of the educational community must discuss and reach agreement on exactly what it is that children should learn and teachers should teach—an essential element in any effort at school reform. Instead, we object to the effort to limit instruction and testing to a narrow range of students' abilities.

Many of the current ideas about testing date back to the early years of the 20th century, when Alfred Binet was asked by the French government to devise a test that would distinguish those children likely to need remedial help from those likely to perform well in school (Gardner, Kornhaber, & Wake, 1996). His "intelligence test" was soon succeeded by the IQ (intelligence quotient) test, which attempts to calculate a child's mental versus chronological age. Over the years, IQ tests have come to be regarded as an all-purpose gauge of an individual's intellectual worth and potential. But in part because of their original task—to predict academic performance—they focus on a narrow band of linguistic and logical-mathematical skills that traditionally have helped students do well academically. Students with strengths in different types of reasoning have little opportunity to demonstrate what they know or can do. Although IQ tests purportedly gauge innate ability rather than achievement, children without access to schooling tend to have lower scores than do children who attend school (Ceci, 1990).

In addition, critics have long pointed out that intelligence tests are culturally biased, requiring a familiarity with the vocabulary, phrasing, and social conventions of the majority culture. An influential 1984 study (Manni, Winikur, & Keller, 1984) showed that a disproportionate number of minority children ended up in remedial classes; most often, these placements were made on the basis of intelligence tests. Unfortunately, many remedial classes do not offer individualized programs, or even the literature and poetry, real-world projects, and hands-on experiments that may enliven a standard curriculum. Instead, they tend to rely on additional drill and worksheets, the kind of activities most likely to bore and frustrate students who already may be uninterested in school.

Furthermore, intelligence tests require individuals to perform mental functions out of context, rather than in the course of normal activity. Experts in a variety of fields have been shown to fail on "formal" measures of the very same calculating or reasoning skills that they use on a daily basis, when tailoring clothes, shopping in a supermarket, or defending their rights in a dispute (Carraher & Schliemann, 1988; Lave, 1980; Rogoff & Lave, 1984; Scribner, 1986). In addition, many traits that individuals use for solving problems—determination, imagination, leadership, social understanding—cannot be addressed by intelligence tests. Other types of standardized tests are designed to measure what students have learned, but they suffer from many of the same shortcomings as do intelligence tests. Standardized tests generally use multiple-choice questions and may be scored by computer, so that only one "right" answer is admissible. The child who thinks creatively and imaginatively, or pauses to think deeply about a question, may not work quickly enough to finish the test. Questions are presented out of context and tend to emphasize recollection of facts, rather than the higher-order thinking and problem-solving skills that children will need for the marketplace of the future.

With the increased mandatory deployment of standardized testing in the schools, we are concerned that very young children will find themselves subjected to high-stakes testing. Although there are valid uses for traditional testing (such as individual clinical diagnosis or determination of causes for poor school performance), for the most part the tests now used to assess young children are of questionable validity (see Meisels, 1989) and often of dubious technical quality.

Results using such instruments tend to be overinterpreted and too easily accepted; scores tend to be given greater weight than is justified. Important educational decisions may be made on the basis of a single score on a single test on a single day. Children may be prevented from entering school, advancing in grade, or participating in special programs, all because of a single score. On the basis of test performance, children have been placed in special education classes, assigned to different schools, or tagged with labels that are difficult or impossible to change. They may be "tracked" into low-level ability groups from which they cannot advance throughout their school career.

Although the routine use of standardized tests most often begins during the elementary years, we are concerned that such testing could have a widespread impact on younger children by exerting a downward pressure for academic instruction. If the performance of a school or school district is judged by student scores on standardized tests, why not start as early as possible to teach the material (or "teach to the test")? When better than the preschool years to inculcate the attitudes and skills that can carry a student forward toward greater and greater heights of academic achievement?

Most psychologists now agree, however, that an academic approach in which the teacher uses lectures, drills, and worksheets to impart knowledge to students is not appropriate for preschool-age children, or even for many older children. Indeed, the most powerful professional organization dealing with early childhood education, the National Association for the Education of Young Children (NAEYC), has produced explicit policy statements cautioning against academically oriented preschool curriculum and instruction (Bredekamp, n.d.).

Under the rubric of "developmentally appropriate practice," the NAEYC argues that young children need broad and pressure-free experience, along with the opportunity to express their own interests and have these interests supported by the adults around them. They need an environment that is "child centered," having as its main agenda that which comes from within the child. Children should not be expected to "perform" or "compete" with other children, but should be protected so that they are able to grow at their own pace (Bredekamp, n.d.).

Our purpose at Spectrum was to develop a kind of alternative assessment compatible with this view of learning in early childhood, one that recognizes the special qualities and abilities that emerge during this period of rapid mental growth, but are likely to be missed with traditional testing methods. We expected that such alternative assessments would be of special importance regarding children of poverty and underrepresented groups, who are negatively affected to a disproportionate degree by standardized testing. We also hoped that more naturalistic forms of assessment would become a powerful tool in educational reform, by pointing out the different and individual ways that all children could learn and succeed.

THE THEORETICAL CONTEXT

So far, I have sketched two different philosophies of education reform: one that strives for academic excellence by setting uniform standards, expecting all children to learn the same material in the same way; another that strives for academic excellence by tailoring the program to students' diverse abilities and ways of learning. Not surprisingly, these two philosophies subscribe to very different brands of assessment and are grounded in divergent theories about the human mind. A complete discussion of 20th-century views of intelligence is well beyond the scope of this book; the reader, however, might find helpful a thumbnail sketch of two important schools of thought: psychometric theory, in which standardized testing has its roots, and cognitive developmental theory, on which our own work is based.

Psychometric theory is built on the belief that intelligence is an inborn, overall, and relatively unchanging trait that can be quantified. One early psychometrician, Francis Galton, believed that intelligence was related to sensory perception and devised mental tests to measure reaction time and hearing. Binet, on the other hand, equated intelligence with "judgment," which he considered a single, "fundamental faculty, the alteration or lack of which, is of the utmost importance for practical life" (Binet & Simon, 1916/1973). Charles Spearman, who conducted his work in England during the early 1900s, proposed that individuals possess a "general intelligence," known as g, which is used to some extent in all intellectual tasks (Spearman, 1904). According to Spearman, g represented an ability to perceive and apply logical relationships in fields as disparate as Latin and music. Although their definitions vary in detail, subsequent psychometricians generally have perceived intelligence as either a unitary faculty or a cluster of faculties (such as reaction time, sensory discrimination, the ability to perceive logical relationships, and memory) that are highly correlated with one another.

Offering evidence of the existence of g, proponents point to the relative consistency of results from one type of intelligence test to another (Herrnstein & Murray, 1994), as well as to other measures of intelligence, such as achievement-test scores, success in school, and status of occupation. Critics suggest that this correlation may reflect test-taking skill rather than a "general intelligence" that encompasses judgment and common sense. Indeed, the correlation is less strong between intelligence-test scores and success in a career (Cronbach, 1990).

Our own theoretical work is built upon a far different view of intelligence, one derived from the work of Jean Piaget (1983), who viewed intelligence as a process of constructing ever more powerful sets of cognitive strutures. Unlike the psychometricians, who were interested in detecting individual differences in intelligence, Piaget wanted to ascertain the principles that govern mental development in all human beings. He viewed intelligence as a universal property, one that develops in a series of qualitatively different stages through which all children progress: sensorimotor, preoperational, concrete operational, and formal operational.

In a series of well-known experiments, Piaget showed that children are not miniature versions of adults, but individuals with mental processes peculiar to their age (Piaget, 1972, 1983). In Piaget's eyes, children are constantly constructing an understanding of the world, holding on to their mental models of the way things work until experimentation and experience convince them otherwise. If an infant learns to look for an object hidden under a pillow, she will keep looking for it there, even if she sees an adult put it somewhere else. A toddler can easily find the object, but is incapable of understanding the principle of conservation of matter; he cannot understand that the quantity of water remains the same when poured into different-sized glasses, or that the amount of clay remains the same when a ball is squashed into a pancake. In similar fashion, a child should not be expected to engage in certain types of abstract thought until she reaches the formal operational stage, usually in early adolescence.

Psychologist Jerome Bruner, with whom Gardner studied at Harvard, took cognitive developmental theory a step further. Whereas in Piaget's view intelligence unfolded automatically, Bruner emphasized the importance of culture in enhancing the natural capabilities of the child (Bruner, Olver, & Greenfield, 1966). In particular, he explored the role that the artifacts, technologies, symbol systems, and literature preserved in a culture can play. Bruner, influenced by another great developmentalist, the Russian Vygotsky (1962, 1978) showed how the availability of tools and highly evolved techniques for using them has irreversibly transformed human development and extended the reach and grasp of human intelligence. (For example, having a thermometer and knowing how to use it allows the provision of crucial information to scientists, physicians, potters, and chefs.) This theoretical work touches on the part that education can play in amplifying individual ability.

For us, the most compelling theoretical issues to be addressed during the 1970s and 1980s revolved around Piaget's universal theory of cognitive development: its core contributions and its limitations. Although Piaget had undertaken the most detailed and far-reaching study of children's mental development of his day, we were troubled by certain aspects of the work. He virtually ignored the arts, focusing almost exclusively on what we conclude to be the logical-mathematical intelligence. He failed to address important issues, including the mechanism by which developmental change occurs; the reasons for diversity among individuals; and the ways in which education can influence development (Feldman, 1980/1994; H. Gardner, 1991). In addition, he postulated that development would occur in all intellectual realms in the same fashion and at the same rate, a concept that Gardner and I would independently explore and later refute.

These limitations notwithstanding, Piaget's theory of cognitive development has advanced the field of psychology by emphasizing the fundamental commonalities in intellectual development that occur in all children in all cultures, regardless of background or environment. Piaget argued for cognitive achievements that are within the grasp of every child. In short, change and transformation make up the core of the developmentalist's credo, and the individual's efforts at achieving these changes constitute the heart of cognitive developmental theory.

Psychometric theory, with its belief in an inborn, unchanging, overall trait that measures intellectual ability, is the most nondevelopmental of all the mainstream perspectives on intelligence. It is not at all surprising then that we who consider ourselves developmentalists would find it hopelessly inadequate as an explanation for intellectual growth and change.

The different ways in which these theories can influence education became clear to us during our years together on a Social Science Research Council committee charged with rejuvenating the study of giftedness and creativity (cf. Feldman, 1982; Feldman, Csikszentmihalyi, & Gardner, 1994). There we found that the psychometric approach to creativity and giftedness had all but stultified real progress in the field. Most often, schools and enrichment programs used intelligence or other types of standardized tests to select candidates for gifted and talented programs, despite a lack of evidence that these tests can detect creativity, motivation, artistic abilities, or other qualities that lead to outstanding performance. Over a period of years we worked together to help shift research in the field from a psychometric to a developmental base, a process still under way (cf. Feldman, 1982; Feldman et al., 1994; Morelock, 1996). Today, researchers (including ourselves) are investigating such issues as the steps by which individuals become excellent at a given endeavor, and the development of assessments, such as portfolios and exhibitions, that identify giftedness by examining an individual's ability to fashion a product or perform in a field of endeavor (Feldman, 1994).

This collaboration helped prepare us for Project Spectrum, a much more ambitious attempt to influence the field of assessment. Nevertheless, the goal was similar: to help move the field away from a psychometric base and toward a cognitive-developmental one (H. Gardner et al., 1996). Within a year of launching the project, we agreed that Spectrum should have its own set of constructs and features and should not be a simple application of either of our theories. To better understand how we forged a middle ground, let us take a brief look at the theories themselves.

Nonuniversal Theory

The perspective that I brought to the project is called nonuniversal theory (Feldman, 1980/1994). It is basically a framework for expanding the field of developmental psychology to better encompass cognitive change that does not occur spontaneously, but requires individual effort and external support—in short, some sort of education. Its central assumption holds that many of the activities pursued by children and adults are developmental but not necessarily universal. By universal, I refer to Piaget's use of the term to describe an inevitable sequence of changes that will be achieved by all individuals, from all backgrounds, under virtually all normal conditions.

Nonuniversal theory proposes that there are many "domains" of activity that are *not* common to all individuals and groups, and that bring with them *no* guarantee of success. Playing the piano and understanding economic theory are two examples. These activities are developmental, in the sense that one needs to reach a certain level of abstract thinking to attempt them; but they are nonuniversal, in the sense that not everyone can (or wants) to perform them competently. Nonuniversal theory argues that most of the time we actually are pursuing expertise in nonuniversal domains. If we want to understand how people choose, engage, pursue, and achieve advanced levels of expertise in nonuniversal domains, we need a framework that does not (as Piaget's does) virtually guarantee that all children eventually will reach the most advanced stage of development (for different views see Ginsburg & Opper, 1988; Piaget, 1972).

Although it was not specifically designed to draw attention to diversity between and among children, groups, and cultures, nonuniversal theory can be used for this purpose—and so it was with Spectrum. The idea of "nonuniversal domains" suggested that there should be numerous and varied opportunities to fulfill individual potential, and that each child should be seen as having distinctive proclivities toward one or more such domains. The goal was not to contradict the central assumption of traditional developmental theory, but rather to enhance and extend some (but not all) of its most powerful assumptions in order to better explain child development.

According to nonuniversal theory, children progress in sequences of levels through domains, or bodies of knowledge and skills (see Figure 1.1). These domains represent developmental achievements that range from *universal*, such as object permanence (knowing that an object still exists

FIGURE 1.1. The Universal to Unique Continuum

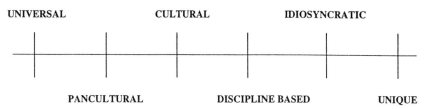

UNIVERSAL   CULTURAL   IDIOSYNCRATIC

PANCULTURAL   DISCIPLINE BASED   UNIQUE

even after it is out of sight), which are virtually guaranteed; to *pancultural*, such as language, which do not need to be taught formally but develop spontaneously in the presence of other human beings; to *cultural*, such as reading, writing, and arithmetic, which all members of our culture are expected to acquire up to a certain level; to *discipline based*, such as in chemistry or law, which are associated with a particular craft, trade, or profession; to *idiosyncratic*, such as in organic chemistry or patent law, which represent specialties and require additional extensive training; to *unique*, such as the discovery of the double helix or the creation of modern dance, which go beyond the existing limits of a domain.

Nonuniversal theory helped provide a framework for determining which intellectual endeavors Project Spectrum would assess. We saw Spectrum as encompassing the middle regions of the universal-to-unique continuum, beginning with cultural domains and extending toward unique domains. Most of the standard school subjects, such as arithmetic and history, fall within the cultural region. But we wanted to take a broader look at children's capacities, identifying unusual interests or abilities in fields that not everyone has the inclination or ability to pursue. Although we did not expect to find 5-year-old naturalists or poets, we did want to figure out how an unusual sensitivity to nature or to expressive use of language might manifest itself in young children.

We ultimately decided to develop assessments in seven domains: language, mathematics, movement, music, science, social understanding, and the visual arts. These domains were selected because of their importance in our culture, and because they represent a range of intelligences as they are expressed in young children. Guided by nonuniversal theory, we saw clearly that our decisions were based on an analysis within a given cultural context; each society might have a different set of domains emerge from its own analysis.

To help children see the link between in-school learning and performance in everyday life, we keyed the Spectrum domains to "endstates," or adult roles valued in our society. (The concept of endstates is shared with

MI theory, where it is one of a number of factors used in defining an intelligence.) A domain found its way into the Spectrum assessments only if we could associate it with an endstate currently well regarded in our culture. When we analyzed the language area, for example, we chose to focus on sets of abilities that may be precursors to three valued endstates: poet, journalist, and writer/storyteller. The goal was not to pigeonhole or label children as future journalists or novelists, but rather to help us focus on those domains in which students could express themselves and perhaps one day make valuable contributions to society.

One of the primary goals of nonuniversal theory is the understanding of transitions, the ways that individuals progress from one developmental level to the next as they acquire expertise (Feldman, 1980/1994, 1986). Since education is about establishing the conditions under which children can achieve mastery and find direction for their future efforts, the relevance of transitions research could not be more direct. Spectrum was intended not only to identify areas of strength in children, but also to provide a base of information about how to enhance positive change. To be sure, this aspect of Spectrum has not yet progressed as far as we had hoped, but remains an important goal.

There are other issues inherent to Spectrum and other assessment efforts that still must be resolved: for example, how should rapid but normal developmental progress be distinguished from extraordinary potential; and how much of a change must occur, and how abruptly, for this change to be considered developmental rather than as a more local, superficial shift in capability. As a developmental theory, nonuniversal theory has helped guide our efforts toward a focus on domains and changes in expertise that are of broad educational significance.

Multiple Intelligences Theory

For most readers, MI theory needs little introduction. Howard Gardner's work on multiple intelligences has become a major topic of discussion in all corners of the education profession. Efforts have been made to apply it to the classroom in a variety of forms, ranging from exercises and tests to policy and scheduling changes. There are few educational areas in which MI theory has not been invoked during the past decade or so, and its important role in educational reform shows no signs of diminishing. For the purposes of this book and other volumes in the Spectrum series, it is not necessary to review MI theory in detail; full-length works are available for that purpose (cf. H. Gardner, 1983/1993, 1993; H. Gardner et al., 1996). A brief summary of the main points, however, may be helpful to the reader, particularly in relation to their impact on Spectrum.

MI theory was intended primarily to expand the range of mental functioning considered under the rubric of *intelligence*. As discussed earlier, intelligence in this country and much of Western culture has tended to be associated with how well one does on an IQ test, an instrument that produces a single score. In recent years, a number of theoreticians have sought new definitions of intelligence. Robert Sternberg of Yale University, for example, has developed a triarchic theory of intelligence in which he analyzes the various information-processing mechanisms that individuals use for problem solving, and also examines the ways that experience influences these mechanisms. Stephen Ceci of Cornell University advances a bioecological view of cognition, which stresses the importance of knowledge and context, rather than an abstract problem-solving ability, in accomplishing intellectual tasks (H. Gardner et al., 1996). Gardner's emphasis has been on the various ways that intelligence manifests itself in different cultures and in different individuals, differences that he contends are based on the fundamental structure of the mind.

Gardner defines intelligence as the "ability to solve problems or fashion products valued by a society." According to MI theory, all individuals possess, to varying degrees, at least seven areas of intellect that function relatively independently. These include the verbal and logical-mathematical abilities found in most IQ tests; musical, spatial, and bodily kinesthetic abilities; and intrapersonal and interpersonal abilities related to the understanding of oneself and others. Gardner recently added an eighth proposed intelligence, that of the naturalist, characterized by a fascination with the natural world (H. Gardner, 1998). It is interesting to note that this domain has been included in the Spectrum array of capabilities since the earliest years of the project, an example of experience in an applied effort eventually impacting theory.

To qualify as an intelligence, each ability had to fare reasonably well in running the gauntlet through a range of criteria. These include the potential for isolated breakdown of the skill through brain damage; the existence of savants, prodigies, and other exceptional individuals with this ability; support from psychological-training studies and from psychometric studies, including correlations across tests; evolutionary plausibility; and a distinct developmental history culminating in a definable set of end-state performances. In addition, each intelligence had to have an identifiable core operation or set of operations, as well as susceptibility to coding in a symbol system (such as language, mathematics, picturing, or musical notes).

Along with nonuniversal theory, MI theory helped frame the areas in which Spectrum tried to assess children's strengths. The domains addressed in the Spectrum battery do not map directly onto the seven intelligences, but reflect the manner in which the intelligences manifest themselves in young children. Furthermore, the intelligences do not operate in isolation; an individual typically must call on several to accomplish a task, such as playing a game of chess or repairing an automobile engine. Performance in a Spectrum domain such as social understanding may call on more than one intelligence (intrapersonal and interpersonal); and a single intelligence (such as spatial) may be exercised in several different domains (visual arts and mechanics and construction). Adjustments also had to be made to translate the intelligences into categories appropriate for schools and easily understood by teachers, parents, and the children themselves, an important goal of Spectrum.

MI theory thus guided Spectrum in a number of other ways. Previous examinations of the symbol systems and "core operations" unique to an intelligence helped us identify the key abilities central to performance in the Spectrum domains. Identification of these core abilities also helped us generate ways in which to support and enrich a child's area of strength both inside and outside of school. MI theory's emphasis on the importance of experience and guided assistance as key to the development of intellectual potential helped us carve out a role for teachers and researchers in advancing the child's own explorations.

As Project Spectrum evolved, it could not help but be swept up in the wave of interest in MI theory. We believe, however, that as the product of two different but complementary theories, Spectrum has made contributions to the assessment and instruction of young children in its own right.

CONCLUDING NOTE

Project Spectrum had as its inspiration a set of frustrations about current educational practice, particularly in the area of testing, and a pair of theories designed to add diversity and richness to the study of intellectual development. The collaboration between its two original architects and the many others who became involved in the enterprise has extended and transformed the original vision of Spectrum in many ways. Throughout its various phases, Spectrum has persisted in its two original aims: to try to broaden conceptions of intellectual potential in young children, and to provide practical techniques for assessing as many of these areas of potential as possible.

These assessments, although never designed to completely replace standardized tests, could provide a supplementary view that reveals the strengths of each child. Earlier in this chapter, I discussed the limitations of standardized testing and the damage that can result from an undue emphasis on its results. Although the alternatives to standardized tests explored in this project may also be criticized and have limitations of their own, they spring from an inherently humane and generous set of beliefs and values, and manifest such values in their design and implementation.

Spectrum assessments have been designed to detect strengths (and, to a lesser extent, areas of weakness) in a way that can be understood and acted upon by parents, teachers, and the children themselves. The intention of the assessments is to assist educators in knowing their students better, in recognizing the great diversity in strengths that exist in youngsters, and in redesigning curricula and instructional approaches. Armed with a better understanding of their students, educators can devise ways to draw on the resources of the school, the home, and the community in order to introduce students to unfamiliar and stimulating realms of knowledge.

Certainly not the only project to have such aims and values, Spectrum has been one effort to contribute to a growing body of knowledge designed to reorient educational practice. This redirection emphasizes a deep and prolonged involvement in challenging bodies of knowledge; a diversity in valued styles of learning; acceptance of differences in talents, abilities, proclivities, and preoccupations; assessment and documentation in familiar contexts and on tasks that have real-world relevance; construction of bridges between the classroom and the community at large; and a commitment to goals shared by all the participants in the educational process.

How far did Spectrum get in achieving those lofty aspirations? How much did it accomplish in efforts at reorientation and reform? How much have its theories and approaches, assessments and techniques influenced practice? These are questions for the wider community to reflect upon and judge. Whatever the judgments turn out to be, we will continue our attempts to improve educational theory, policy, and practice in the firm belief that such efforts can make a difference.

REFERENCES

Binet, A., & Simon, T. (1973). *The development of intelligence in children (the Binet-Simon Scale)* (Elizabeth S. Kite, Trans.). New York: Arno Press. (Original work published 1916)

Bredekamp, S. (Ed.) (n.d.) *NAEYC position statement on developmentally appropriate practice in early childhood programs serving children from birth through age 8.* Washington, DC: National Association for the Education of Young Children.

Bruner, J. S., Olver, R. R., & Greenfield, P. M. (1966). *Studies in cognitive growth.* New York: John Wiley.

Carraher, T. N. & Schliemann, A. D. (1988). Culture, arithmetic, and mathematical models. *Cultural Dynamics, 1,* 180–194.

Ceci, S. J. (1990). *On intelligence . . . more or less: A bio-ecological treatise on intellectual development.* Englewood Cliffs, NJ: Prentice Hall.

Cronbach, L. J. (1990). *Essentials of psychological testing.* New York: Harper & Row.

Feldman, D. H. (Ed.). (1982). *Developmental approaches to giftedness and creativity.* San Francisco: Jossey-Bass.

Feldman, D. H. (1991). *Nature's gambit: Child prodigies and the development of human potential.* New York: Teachers College Press. (Original work published 1986)

Feldman, D. H. (1980/1994). *Beyond universals in cognitive development* (2nd ed.). Norwood, NJ: Ablex.

Feldman, D. H., Csikszentmihalyi, M., & Gardner, H. (1994). *Changing the world: A framework for the study of creativity.* Westport, CT: Greenwood Press.

Gardner, D. (Ed.). (1983). *A nation at risk.* Washington, DC: U.S. Department of Education.

Gardner, H. (1991). *The unschooled mind: How children think and how schools should teach.* New York: Basic Books.

Gardner, H. (1993). *Frames of mind: The theory of multiple intelligences.* New York: Basic Books. (Original work published 1983)

Gardner, H. (1993). *Multiple intelligences: The theory in practice.* New York: Basic Books.

Gardner, H. (1998). Are there additional intelligences? In J. Kane (Ed.), *Education, information, and transformation* (pp. 111–131). Englewood Cliffs, NJ: Prentice Hall.

Gardner, H., Kornhaber, M., & Wake, W. (1996). *Intelligence: Multiple perspectives.* Ft. Worth, TX: Harcourt Brace.

Ginsburg, H., & Opper, S. (1988). *Piaget's theory of intellectual development* (3rd ed.). Englewood Cliffs, NJ: Prentice Hall.

Herrnstein, R. J., & Murray, C. (1994). *The bell curve: Intelligence and class structure in American life.* New York: Free Press.

Lave, J. (1980). What's special about experiments as contexts for thinking? *Quarterly Newsletter of the Laboratory of Comparative Human Cognition, 2,* 86–91.

Manni, J. L., Winikur, D. W., & Keller, M. R. (1984). *Intelligence, mental retardation, and the culturally different child: A practitioner's guide.* Springfield, IL: Thomas.

Meisels, S. J. (1989). High-stakes testing in kindergarten. *Educational Leadership, 46,* 16–22.

Morelock, M. J. (1996). On the nature of giftedness and talent: Imposing order on chaos. *Roeper Review, 19,* 4–12.

Piaget, J. (1972). Intellectual evolution from adolescence to adulthood. *Human Development, 15,* 1–12.

Piaget, J. (1983). Piaget's theory. In P. Mussen (Ed.), *Manual of child psychology* (pp. 103–128). New York: John Wiley.

Rogoff, B. & Lave, J. (Eds.). (1984). *Everyday cognition: Its development in social context.* Cambridge, MA: Harvard University Press.

Schön, D. A. (1983). *The reflective practitioner: How professionals think in action.* New York: Basic Books.

Scribner, S. (1986). Thinking in action: Some characteristics of practical thought. In R. J. Sternberg and R. K. Wagner (Eds.), *Practical intelligence: Nature and origins of competence in the everyday world.* Cambridge, UK: Cambridge University Press.

Slavin, R. E., Karweit, N. L., & Madden, N. A. (Eds.). (1989). *Effective programs for students at risk.* Boston: Allyn & Bacon.

Spearman, C. (1904). General intelligence, objectively determined and measured. *American Journal of Psychology, 15,* 201–293.

Sternberg, R. (1985). *Beyond IQ: A triarchic theory of human intelligence.* Cambridge, UK: Cambridge University Press.

Vygotsky, L. S. (1962). *Thought and language.* Cambridge, MA: MIT Press.

Vygotsky, L. S. (1978). *Mind in society: The development of higher psychological processes.* Cambridge, MA: Harvard University Press.

CHAPTER 2

ILLUMINATING CHILDREN'S MINDS

What would it really mean to attend to children's individual differences? Consider the following two profiles of children who participated in Project Spectrum during the 3rd year of the project's collaboration with the Eliot-Pearson Children's School, a laboratory preschool affiliated with the Eliot-Pearson Department of Child Development at Tufts University.

At age 3 years, 7 months, Kira[1] is the youngest child in her preschool class of 20 students. Yet she approaches each of the Spectrum activities with confidence and determination. In creative movement, she reveals an unusual sensitivity to different kinds of music. While listening to folk music, she performs an expressive dance by moving only her shoulders and hips back and forth in graceful curving motions. When faster music is played, she moves her whole body, shaking her head and arms in time to the beat. Even when other children choose not to dance, Kira continues on her own, moving freely about the room.

Kira demonstrates similar ability in athletic movement. She frequently offers to show her classmates new gymnastic moves and encourages them to challenge themselves athletically with cartwheels and somersaults. During an outdoor obstacle course activity, she walks swiftly across a balance beam and runs easily around obstacles.

During group times, Kira often knows the lyrics to the songs and sings clearly and loudly. On the Spectrum music production activity, Kira maintains a consistent tempo while singing "Happy Birthday" and generally stays in tune. During the music perception activity, she accurately identifies subtle errors in a familiar tune and identifies two other tunes after hearing only a few notes of each. It is clear that Kira takes great pleasure in her singing—indeed during the storytelling activity, she sings most of her story.

Eric is Kira's classmate and this is his second year in a Spectrum classroom. He exhibits strengths in art, numbers, and logical inference. Eric demonstrates unusual representational ability in the visual arts. His drawings contain elaborate and telling detail, and he places his figures and shapes carefully on the page. Eric covers a range of imaginative themes in his work: One drawing shows a magician with two rabbits coming out of a hat and a clown's head taking the place of a sun. Another drawing shows two turtles in baseball caps running a race. Eric also demonstrates an unusual command of perspective. He often draws profiles of people and animals, and he seems to be exploring the notion of "occlusion" (partial obstruction) in his work. One drawing depicts a car in a garage, but the only part of the car that we see is its smoking tailpipe. In another drawing, a cat is chasing a mouse toward its mouse hole, but only the cat's large underbelly and its front legs are visible.

Eric also displays a solid understanding of notational systems. While playing a board game that fosters adding and subtracting skills, he uses colored chips to keep track of small figures getting on and off a toy bus at different stops. He uses green chips to represent the adults and blue chips to represent the children boarding and exiting the bus. Even without the chips, Eric is able to make accurate mental calculations of how many people are riding the bus. During a treasure hunt game, Eric makes accurate predictions about where to find the treasures hidden under different colored flags. After the game, he successfully identifies the rule governing the placement of objects in treasure boxes, including the more abstract association that certain treasure boxes will always be empty.

In general, Eric's approach to the Spectrum activities is serious and focused, but somewhat tentative. In art, he often reworks a painting or drawing if the first one does not achieve the effect he intended. As the year progresses, Eric becomes more comfortable with the Spectrum staff, initiating conversations with the adults that allow him to explore his ideas more fully.

What distinguishes these portraits of Kira and Eric? We believe that they provide unusually detailed insight into Kira's abilities in creative and athletic movement and music production and perception, and into the various dimensions of Eric's artistic ability—his sense of perspective, attention to composition, and use of detail. To be sure, any good teacher provides a range of materials and activities in his or her classroom. Teachers who are artistic may spend more time enriching the art resources, whereas musically inclined teachers might introduce a variety of exotic instruments. When observing children, they may refer to which of a child's paintings they especially like or who is always first to play the new instrument.

But even these teachers tend to focus on their students' language and math abilities when talking about cognitive development, seldom mentioning strengths in the music, movement, or visual art domains. Furthermore, their observations often remain at a generalized level. They may describe children in terms of broad, universal stages of cognitive, social-emotional, or physical development, without attempting to determine more carefully individual differences within each of these areas of development.

In this chapter, we present an approach to assessment that looks at young children more broadly as well as more deeply than do many traditional measures. Rather than situating the Spectrum assessment framework in the world of short-answer tests, we ground our assessments solidly in the world of experiences available to children both inside and outside the classroom. The Spectrum framework encourages teachers to think of children and their work and work products in new ways. The initial hypothesis of the project was that most children—whether or not they would be considered "gifted" in a traditional sense—will demonstrate a distinctive profile or cast of mind if they are presented with a broad enough set of experiences. By shining a wider and brighter light on children and their activities and products, we hope to illuminate more of the potential of children's minds and to increase the likelihood that they will realize their potential both in and outside of school.

DESIGNING THE ASSESSMENTS

Assessment in most preschool classrooms is relatively informal. Teachers may make observations, but rarely in a systematic way. If they team teach, teachers will often discuss individual children with one another. They also may fill out developmental checklists or write brief narrative reports that include anecdotal information and observations of children in the different areas of the classroom. Sometimes teachers devise their own informal assessment formats or borrow them from published materials. If a teacher is concerned about a particular child, the teacher often will make a referral for a more formal evaluation, which almost always is designed to look at deficits. The areas targeted are usually language and communication issues, behavioral or emotional problems, or pervasive developmental delays. Although intelligence tests are not administered routinely at the preschool level, when they are, they typically include a series of tasks that assess children's verbal, spatial, and numerical abilities. Scores on these tests are considered indicators of children's abilities to reason, think, and solve problems.

Against this backdrop, our team of researchers at Harvard University's Project Zero and the Tufts Eliot-Pearson Department of Child Development took on the challenge of creating an alternative approach to assessment in early childhood. The original team consisted of Tufts researchers David Henry Feldman and Janet Stork and Harvard researchers Howard Gardner, Mara Krechevsky, and Ulla Malkus.

Whereas Feldman and Gardner brought the power of their theories, Stork and Malkus brought years of experience as preschool teachers. Malkus, who had a flair for curriculum design, was interested in applying a multiple intelligences approach to classroom instruction. Stork, who had directed an early-education program, wanted to explore the role of the teacher in promoting children's development, an area that she felt was not addressed adequately by Piagetian theory. The fifth member of the team, who steered the project through to its final days, was Krechevsky. She brought a background in psychology and a strong interest in studying development in the arts. She joined the project in order to investigate how MI theory could be translated into assessment instruments that would work in schools.[2]

Because of its affiliation with Tufts University, we chose the Eliot-Pearson Children's School as the place where we would put our ideas to the test. Located in Medford, Massachusetts, the laboratory school is a low-slung brick building, with large, open classrooms. Medford is an urban-suburban, low- to middle-income community, with pockets of ethnic diversity including Irish American, Italian American, and African American families. The school has a long-standing philosophy of active learning and progressive education and a strong belief in the inclusion of children with special needs. In the mid-1980s, Eliot-Pearson offered half-day programs for 3- and 4-year-old children and a parent–toddler program. The children in the programs lived primarily in the surrounding community and came from white, middle-income families.

In the early days, the Spectrum team traveled back and forth between Tufts and Harvard, holding meetings in Gardner's and Feldman's offices, and sometimes in the 15-minute car rides between Cambridge and Medford. We shared a belief that schools were not serving children well because the conventional views of intelligence were too narrow. We wanted to develop a set of assessments that focused explicitly on identifying children's strengths, that expanded the domains being assessed to more than just language and math, and that were closely linked to roles and products that both adults and children would recognize as meaningful. Kira's and Eric's profiles offer a glimpse of that vision.

Furthermore, we believed that given a favorable environment, children might exhibit strengths and gifts that previously had not been detected. Feldman and Gardner independently had been studying prodigies and other exceptional individuals, and were impressed by the way that family, cultural, and even historical forces had to converge for an individual to exhibit great talent in his or her field—a situation called co-incidence (Feldman, 1986/1991). According to this view, an individual is not gifted because of heredity alone, nor because of environment or training alone, but because of a constant and complex interaction among these forces that leads to the attainment of competence or even greatness (Gardner, Hatch, & Torff, 1997). We wanted to create the kind of classroom culture in which children could show their strengths.

We started the project by determining which domains of development we wished to address, a process described in the previous chapter. Although we used the seven intelligences as our starting point, we soon digressed from addressing "intelligences" per se to tapping abilities in the context of domains, or bodies of knowledge, explored in a preschool class.

Each member of our group took responsibility for a different domain of development as we strove to identify the criteria, or key abilities, most worthy of assessment. We wanted to select competencies that could be observed in preschoolers, that individual children would exhibit to varying degrees, and that had readily apparent links to adult competencies of consequence. In addition to conducting extensive classroom observations, we surveyed the research literature and consulted regularly with both our teacher-collaborators and subject matter experts (educational researchers in each domain) to identify the range of abilities exhibited by preschool children over the course of the year.

Next, we had to fashion the assessment instruments or tasks. In some content areas, including music, math, and language, we used as a point of departure the tasks already developed for the Project Zero Early Symbolization Project.[3] In other areas, we examined relevant tests and games and materials already in use in the classroom, and built upon tasks designed by other investigators for curriculum or research purposes. In order to observe children engaged in all different types of activities, we visited preschool programs in the Boston area that exemplified different educational approaches, including Montessori and Waldorf schools and the local children's and science-discovery museums.

Using all of this information, we developed and pilot tested a series of activities with individual children. Translating our ideas from theory and research into practice was not easy; we strayed down many unpromising paths. Originally, we had intended to use a variety of diagnostic approaches in each domain. But one approach proved far more successful than the others: allowing children to interact with appealing materials, such as a water table or sets of bells, and observing their level of interest and skill. The hands-on activities not only captured the children's attention, but also highlighted differences in children's abilities in a dramatic way. As a result of our experiences in the field, we decided to focus exclusively on "authentic" assessments that evaluated children in the context of their work.

Over time, we devised a set of task criteria to guide us in designing the assessments. For example, we wanted the activities to fit easily into the classroom context, use readily available materials, and be engaging and meaningful for 4-year-olds. We also designed the tasks to reflect significant adult roles and competencies in our society. Therefore, we looked at abilities important for singers, reporters, and naturalists, among others, by asking children to sing a birthday song, report news about their weekend, and observe seasonal changes and other natural phenomena. In each case, we examined key abilities in the context of an activity that was relevant to the child.

Our approach also reflected a belief that children learn best through regular interaction with stimulating materials. We hoped that with the right kinds of materials, activities, and adult guidance, children would reveal what they liked and were good at. Hence, we tried to blur the line dividing curriculum and assessment by collecting information over time in the child's own setting. The Spectrum materials could be used as instruments for learning as well as for assessment, and most of them resembled other activities in the preschool classroom.

Finally, we tried to use measures that are what we call "intelligence-fair." We rejected the assessment tradition of looking at all abilities through the lenses of language or logic, as so many short-answer and pencil-and-paper tests do. In Spectrum, children work directly with the materials and information of a domain, rather than simply answer questions about a content area. For example, children play actual musical instruments for the music-perception measure, and conduct their own simple sink-and-float experiments for the hypothesis-testing measure.

After 2 years of extensive field-testing at Eliot-Pearson, we were ready to use our instruments to assess children in a systematic way. We brought with us to the classroom 15 assessments in seven domains, ranging from structured games in math and science to open-ended exploration with paint and other media. We also devised scoring systems and a method for reporting our results to parents and the research community. We were at last prepared to discover the unique strengths in every child.

PUTTING THE THEORY TO THE TEST

"We're trying to create a world of persons and objects that elicits children's distinctive strengths." This was how Gardner eventually came to describe our undertaking. We hoped to provide a rich and evocative environment that would engage children in different domains and reveal how individual children's minds worked in ways we otherwise might not see. We had three guiding research questions: (a) Did young children exhibit domain-specific as well as more general strengths? (b) Were there significant correlations between children's performances on different activities? and (c) Did the Spectrum assessments identify strengths that teachers and parents did not recognize? In one class, we also compared the results of 10 of the Spectrum activities to the Stanford-Binet Intelligence Scale (4th ed.).

The assessments that we developed covered not only language and mathematics, but also movement, visual arts, music, science, and social understanding (see Appendix A). Within each domain, we examined at least two key abilities (abilities that we considered essential for performing tasks in the domain). In science, for example, we looked at experimental, naturalist, and mechanical abilities, and in the social domain, we looked at children's interactions with peers as well as their understanding of social dynamics in the classroom.

During the design stage of the project, we had observed that working style—such as the motivation, confidence, or persistence with which a child tackled an activity—had a significant effect on outcome. So we decided to monitor the way in which children approached activities in different content areas to determine whether these stylistic tendencies varied or remained constant across domains (see Figure 2.1 for a list of working styles). In keeping with MI theory, we were loathe to generalize about children's abilities to show focus, persistence, or reflectiveness in the absence of observing them engage in a variety of experiences.

Throughout the year, we met weekly with the Eliot-Pearson teachers and reviewed each assessment activity so that the teachers could introduce them comfortably to the children. We also talked about classroom setup and management issues, but because of our research question contrasting assessment results with teacher observations, we did not reveal what we were learning about the children. We launched the assessments at the end of September, starting with a math activity called the Dinosaur Game and ending with a specially designed obstacle course in April.

Administering the Assessments

Although the assessment activities are described elsewhere in detail (Krechevsky, 1998), it might be helpful here to take a closer look at one activity, Assembly, to see how the evaluation process worked. In this task, we examined children's ability to understand the relationship between different parts of a simple machine by asking them to take apart and re-

FIGURE 2.1. Working Styles Checklist

Child _____   Observer _____

Activity _____   Date _____

Please mark which working styles are distinctive during your observation. Mark only when obvious; one from each pair need not be checked. Please include comments and anecdotes whenever possible and write a general, overall phrase that best describes how the child approached the activity. Star (*) any outstanding working style.

Child is

easily engaged in activity	_____	persistent	_____
reluctant to engage in activity	_____	frustrated by task	_____
confident	_____	impulsive	_____
tentative	_____	reflective	_____
playful	_____	apt to work slowly	_____
serious	_____	apt to work quickly	_____
focused	_____	conversational	_____
distractible	_____	quiet	_____

Comments:

_____

responds to visual _____ auditory _____ kinesthetic _____ cues

demonstrates planful approach

brings personal strength to activity

finds humor in content area

uses materials in unexpected ways

shows pride in accomplishment

attends to detail; is observant

is curious about materials

shows concern over "correct" answer

focuses on interaction with adult

assemble a food grinder. Acting on our belief that children need experience in a content area in order to demonstrate potential in that area,
teachers gave the children time to play with large wooden nuts and bolts,
hinges and door knobs, and other simple hardware for a few weeks before
the assessment. At group time, the teacher read books to the children
about machines and tools. After that, she brought out the food grinders
and told children that over the next few days they would be able to play
with different kinds of gadgets that could be taken apart and put back
together. Children eagerly signed up for their turn with the new machines.

At a small table behind the bookshelf, Krechevsky, one of the Spectrum researchers, conducted the 15- to 20-minute activity with each child.
Children were easily engaged and generated many ideas about what the
grinder might be, including "a gas compressor," "a water fountain," and
something that "makes tuna fish." If children could not identify the object,
Krechevsky explained that it was a food grinder and told them to look at
it carefully because after taking the grinder apart, they would need to put
it back together.

Once the children began the task, striking differences in their abilities
and styles of problem solving began to emerge. Some children, such as
Kira, had difficulty understanding how the parts fit together. After twirl-
ing the handle a few times, she identified the main fastener, unscrewed it,
and proceeded quickly to disassemble the rest of the grinder, including
removing the handle from the inner spiral core. But putting the grinder
back together presented a greater challenge. Kira began well by replacing
the spiral core, but then became confused about which piece should be put
on next. She tried a somewhat random trial-and-error approach, putting
washers on before gears and repeatedly trying to put the handle on back-
wards. Krechevsky gave Kira increasingly greater support so that she
would have the experience of completing the task successfully.

Christie, on the other hand, breezed through the exercise without any
adult guidance. When she was puzzled, she could use a trial-and-error
approach to put the pieces back. Gordon worked systematically, and even
was able to explain why different parts fit together in terms of their function. Tricia became distracted when she saw all the pieces laid out in front
of her, but settled down when Krechevsky helped her focus on one piece
at a time. Other children, such as Nicky, lacked the fine motor skills
needed to manipulate the parts easily and needed support throughout
the task.

A second Spectrum researcher, Valerie Ramos-Ford, acted as observer, recording this wide array of behaviors using an individual observation sheet for each child. She awarded children one to three points on a

list of categories, including sense of parts to whole, problem solving, attention to detail, and fine motor skills. She also noted the level of support or scaffolding that children needed and their working styles. Each child's observation sheet was added to a growing folder that included documentation from all of the assessments, in the form of either structured scoresheets or observational checklists.

Although we developed quantitative scoring systems for research purposes, we never reported numerical scores to parents. Rather, we used the information collected on children's performances and products throughout the year to compose a one- to two-page narrative for each child. These "profiles," as shown in the opening sketches of Kira and Eric, described each child's strengths, in terms of either his or her cognitive profile or of the class as a whole.

To help parents follow up on the information contained in the profiles, we created an activities manual and a community resource list, both of which were categorized by domain. In Kira's case, we wrote that she might benefit from some of the assembly activities described in the manual, which included using basic tools and hardware, making vehicles out of Legos, creating inventions out of recycled materials, and making puzzles out of cardboard. Although activities sometimes were suggested in order to offer children experience in a wide variety of areas or help them in areas of difficulty, more often, they were intended to help parents nurture and encourage an area of strength. However, we cautioned parents that although the profiles focused on strengths, they should be interpreted as *de*scriptions rather than as *pre*scriptions. Identifying children's areas of interest can be just as important as identifying their strengths.

Research Results

We conducted assessments such as the Assembly Activity with every child in the Spectrum class and analyzed our results in terms of our initial research questions. We found that the Spectrum assessments did identify distinct intellectual profiles for the majority of children (for a full discussion, see Gardner & Hatch, 1989; Krechevsky & Gardner, 1990). Every child exhibited at least one strength, if not in the context of his or her peer group, then in the context of his or her own cognitive profile. Moreover, there was little correlation between children's performances on the different activities; only the two math activities, involving related number concepts, were significantly correlated.

Because of the small sample size (39 subjects), our results must be regarded as tentative. We hope that other researchers will build on this work and conduct reliability and validity studies so that norms can be established. Margaret Adams, while a doctoral candidate in the Tufts Department of Child Development, took important steps in this direction. She administered modified versions of six of the assessments (the Assembly task plus one activity each in the domains of language, math, music, visual arts, and social understanding) to 42 subjects ages 4.2 to 4.8 years. She, too, found that children exhibited strengths and weaknesses across the domains, rather than a uniform level of ability; furthermore, no two cognitive profiles were alike (Adams, 1993).[4]

As for our own study, there were other findings of note. Some children had such strong affinities for particular domains that they transformed activities in other domains to conform to their own strengths and interests. Seth, who enjoyed storytelling, transformed the Sink and Float Activity into a story about the "great and famous sponge man." Sarah transported her language skills to the art table by making decorative drawings for the stories she invented, and also used the Classroom Model (a measure of social understanding) and Bus Game activities (math) as occasions to create stories.

This type of response to the activities (which in some classroom situations might be dismissed as a failure to follow directions) could have educational implications. We found that some children were able to use their strengths to improve performance in other domains. For instance, Ben, a boy with unusual singing abilities but less interest in creative movement, moved more rhythmically when he sang. Ben also embellished the story he told for the Storyboard Activity by inventing a theme song and a funeral dirge to accompany the actions of his characters. Ideally, Ben might continue to use his musical abilities as an entry point to challenging material in school. For example, he might make up songs to express the mood of a piece of literature, or learn about fractions by studying different rhythmic patterns.

In regard to our research question comparing results on the Spectrum assessments with teacher and parent questionnaires, we found that Spectrum identified strengths in science, music, visual arts, and social understanding that had not been identified by either parent or teacher. Parents were most surprised to learn of strengths in music perception, mechanical ability, and creative movement. Whereas it is relatively easy for teachers and parents to identify ability in such areas as language and math, ability in areas such as mechanical skills and music perception may be missed.

The comparison of Spectrum results with subscores on the Stanford-Binet Intelligence Scale yielded only weak correlations. For the most part, performance on the Stanford-Binet was not predictive of performance either across or on specific subsets of the Spectrum activities, except for a possible connection between Stanford-Binet composite scores and the

Spectrum music assessments. Because of the small sample size (we conducted the Stanford-Binet test with 17 children in one class), these results
must be regarded as tentative. Nevertheless, the possible correlation is
fascinating in light of recent research by Rauscher and her colleagues
(Rauscher et al., 1997), showing that serious study of a musical instrument
during the preschool years helps to prepare students for some of the disci-
plinary and notational demands of school.

A COMPARATIVE VIEW OF EARLY CHILDHOOD EDUCATION

How does the Spectrum model compare to other approaches in early
childhood education? Because it weaves together curriculum and assessment, Spectrum does not easily fit into the traditional categories. Nevertheless, we will try to describe the landscape so that readers may better
understand where Spectrum is situated.

Approaches to Curriculum

At first glance, Spectrum seems unrelated to more didactic models that
focus on direct instruction in skills and facts and on preparing children to
meet the traditional academic (language and math) objectives that await
them in elementary school (Bereiter & Engelmann, 1966). But the approach does not fit easily with "emergent curriculum" models either, in
which curriculum is largely determined by children's interests, and prior
knowledge and the role of the adult is minimized (but cf. Edwards, Gandini, & Forman, 1993). At its best, the Spectrum framework serves as a
bridge between the academic and more child-centered approaches to early
education. It is designed to foster cognitive skills in a systematic way, but
expands what we think of as cognitive skills to include many different
domains.

We will start our brief survey by comparing Spectrum to two widespread curriculum approaches in early childhood education, the Montessori method and the project-based model.

The Montessori Method. Maria Montessori (1964) believed that children
learn through their senses; therefore, she created a set of materials to increase children's sensitivity to their environment and to encourage their
ability to make sense of their experience. She developed, along with sensory materials, didactic materials to prepare children for more-academic
skills such as reading, writing, and math, as well as practical life materials

to foster children's autonomy in such tasks as buttoning buttons or tying laces (Feinburg & Mindess, 1994). The Montessori materials are presented in a predetermined order and are all designed to be self-correcting. Today, the Montessori method is practiced both in its original form, as sponsored by the International Montessori Society, and in a more updated form, as sponsored by the American Montessori Society.

Although Spectrum, like Montessori, emphasizes the use of rich and evocative materials from a wide variety of domains, the Spectrum activities are more open ended and less prescriptive. Many of the Spectrum assessments do not presuppose one way, or a right or wrong way, in which to use the materials. Children can tell many different kinds of stories for the Storyboard Activity or generate many different experiments for the Sink and Float Activity. Although some of the Spectrum materials can be considered self-correcting, such as reassembling the food grinder or calculating the number of people riding a bus, most of the Spectrum assessments include a free-play component as well.

In most Montessori programs, a greater emphasis is placed on using the materials in particular ways than on fostering children's creativity, cooperative planning, imaginative play, or group projects (Greenberg, 1990). Although Montessori had great respect for children and their autonomy, she believed that a sense of order was necessary in order for children to be creative. The Montessori materials typically are presented in a carefully sequenced series of activities through which children progress at their own pace under the watchful eye of the teacher. Each of the sensory materials focuses on only one of the senses; when a particular sensory organ is involved, the other sensory stimuli are often isolated. Although the Spectrum materials are designed to help identify abilities in particular domains, children are encouraged to explore the materials freely using their multiple senses, and evidence of proclivities other than those that the activity is intended to tap is always noted.

Thus, like Montessori, Spectrum emphasizes children's active involvement in learning, individualizing the curriculum, and the importance of a "prepared" environment. But the Spectrum teacher's role is less regulatory with regard to the use of materials and workspace and the materials generally are less prescriptive.

Project-Based Models. Spectrum is perhaps closest in philosophy to constructivist and project-based models in the tradition of Piaget and Dewey (see Katz & Chard, 1989). These approaches encourage children to create meaning through interactions with the physical and social worlds. As noted earlier, most of the Spectrum assessments are situated in real-life activities and engage children in a variety of problem-solving tasks. Projects also provide a real-life context for learning and practicing language, math, and other skills.

Katz and Chard (1989) define projects as in-depth studies about various topics that are carried out by small groups of children. They see projects as promoting four kinds of learning goals: *knowledge* (e.g., facts, concepts, ideas, vocabulary), *skills* (e.g., learning to read, count, or manipulate objects), *dispositions* (habits of mind or tendencies to respond to situations in certain ways, e.g., curiosity or friendliness), and *feelings* (subjective emotional states such as feelings of belonging or competence). Projects help children gain a deeper understanding of the events and phenomena in their surrounding environment while allowing them to make decisions and choices about the course of their own learning.

Like Spectrum, most project-based approaches emphasize the importance of documenting children's work (see Edwards, Gandini, & Forman, 1993). But projects often involve more active planning, implementing, and evaluating *with* children than do the Spectrum activities. Projects entail more in-depth explorations of a topic over time, such as exploring a supermarket or studying a school bus or a construction site. They also often use a more integrated or interdisciplinary approach to teaching and learning. Unlike Spectrum, project work does not typically highlight the disciplines. For instance, most projects do not provide a framework for thinking about, nurturing, and assessing key abilities in a discipline. Instead, disciplines such as art or movement may be employed as vehicles for teaching or expressing something else. Some classroom teachers choose to combine the two approaches—for example, by trying to include activities in each of the Spectrum domains in the course of conducting a project.

The Bank Street developmental-interactionist model (Shapiro & Biber, 1972) is similar in many respects to the project model. Both approaches emphasize connecting children's in-school experiences with real-world situations. The Bank Street model is based on giving children concrete experiences and actively engaging children in the selection and use of learning materials. Perhaps the main difference between Bank Street and Spectrum is that Bank Street stresses looking at the "whole child" and integrating cognitive and affective development as much as possible, whereas Spectrum focuses on the cognitive aspects of development.

Approaches to Assessment

As noted earlier, many preschool programs do not have formal systems for assessing children. In recent years, however, two new assessment intruments were published that were designed expressly for use with young

FIGURE 2.2. Spectrum Assessment Categories [Adapted from Krechevsky, M. (1998). *Project Spectrum: Preschool Assessment Handbook.* New York: Teachers College Press.]

MOVEMENT
- Creative Movement Measure:
  Biweekly Movement
  Curriculum
- Athletic Movement Measure:
  Obstacle Course

VISUAL ARTS
- Art Portfolio:
  Yearlong collection of
  children's artwork
  supplemented by
  structured activities

LANGUAGE
- Invented Narrative Measure:
  Storyboard Activity
- Descriptive Narrative Measure
  Reporter Activities

SOCIAL
- Social Analysis Measure:
  Classroom Model
- Social Roles Measure:
  Peer Interaction
  Checklist

SCIENCE
- Naturalist Measure:
  Discovery Area
- Logical Inference Measure:
  Treasure Hunt Game
- Hypothesis-Testing Measure:
  Sink and Float Activity
- Mechanical Measure:
  Assembly Activity

MUSIC
- Production Measures:
  Happy Birthday
  New Songs—
   Up in the Air
   Animal Song
- Perception Measures:
  Pitch Matching Games
  Song Recognition

MATHEMATICS
- Counting/Strategy Measure:
  Dinosaur Game
- Calculating/Notation Measure:
  Bus Game

WORKING STYLES
- Working Style Checklist

children: the Work Sampling System (Meisels, 1993; Meisels, 1994) and the High/Scope Child Observation Record (High/Scope Educational Research Foundations, 1992). Like Spectrum, they both shun testlike situations and instead give teachers guidelines for observing children as they work.

FIGURE 2.3. Work Sampling System Assessment Categories [Adapted from Jablon, J.R. et al. (1994). *Omnibus Guidelines, Preschool through Third Grade* (3rd ed.). Ann Arbor, MI: Rebus Planning Associates.]

I. Personal and Social Development
A. Self-concept
B. Self-control
C. Approach to learning
D. Interaction with others
E. Conflict resolution

II. Language and Literacy
A. Listening
B. Speaking
C. Literature and reading
D. Writing
E. Spelling

III. Mathematical Thinking
A. Approach to mathematical thinking
B. Patterns and relationships
C. Number concept and operations
D. Geometry and spatial relations
E. Measurement
F. Probability and statistics

IV. Scientific Thinking
A. Observing and investigating
B. Questioning and predicting
C. Explaining and forming conclusions

V. Social Studies
A. Human similarities and differences
B. Human interdependence
C. Rights and responsibilities
D. People and where they live
E. People and the past

VI. The Arts
A. Expression and representation
B. Artistic appreciation

VII. Physical Development
A. Gross motor development
B. Fine motor development
C. Personal health and safety

The Work Sampling System. The Work Sampling System (WSS) was developed by Samuel Meisels and his colleagues in response to the lack of appropriate assessments for children from age 3 to Grade 5. The WSS is a performance assessment that includes three complementary components: developmental guidelines with a two-page checklist, which teachers must complete for each student three times a year; portfolios of children's work, collected over the course of the year and providing a way to monitor individual growth; and teachers' summary reports, also completed three times a year, which build on the developmental checklists and portfolios. By combining these different measures, the WSS aims "to document and assess children's skills, knowledge, behavior, and accomplishments across a wide variety of classroom activities and areas of learning on multiple occasions" (Meisels et al., 1994, p. 4).

At first glance, the WSS assessment categories appear somewhat similar to those of Spectrum (see Figures 2.2 and 2.3). However, the foundations are very different. WSS is solidly grounded in developmentally appropriate classroom practice, whereas Spectrum is based on Feldman's and Gardner's theoretical claims that human cognition is pluralistic and domain specific. If we return for a moment to Feldman's continuum of universal-to-unique development, the WSS targets developmental milestones in the cultural domains, which all children are expected to achieve (e.g., counting up to 5 or communicating clearly enough to be understood by others). In contrast, Spectrum focuses on the strengths and proclivities that are unique to an individual and may extend into the discipline-based or idiosyncratic domains.

The WSS areas of assessment are based on seven current curricular areas in early childhood education: personal and social development, language and literacy, mathematical thinking, scientific thinking, social studies, the arts, and physical development. The checklists for these areas reflect actual classroom goals and objectives. They incorporate information from a wide range of sources, including local, state, and national standards for curriculum development. In contrast, the Spectrum activities were designed in light of adult roles that are considered meaningful in our society, and the abilities needed to step into these roles. Interestingly enough, these different pathways sometimes led to similar assessment criteria; for example, both approaches recommend looking at children's responses to music and of their use of lines and shapes, important skills for dancers and artists, respectively, as well as widespread components of the early childhood curriculum. (For samples of the two approaches, see Figures 2.4 and 2.5.)

In sum, the WSS has much to recommend it. This program provides a means for systematically documenting children's growth and development from ages 3 to 10; offers professional development procedures and materials; and has established internal reliability, interrater reliability, and comparisons to norm-referenced measures (Meisels, Liaw, & Nelson, 1995). Spectrum, on the other hand, offers a curricular component, in line with the belief that children need to be presented with information and materials from different domains before their cognitive abilities and potentials can be assessed adequately.

The High/Scope Child Observation Record. Like the WSS, the High/Scope Child Observation Record (COR) is designed to chart children's growth and development over time. It is intended for use with children ages 2½ to 6 years. Although the COR was originally developed to accompany the High/Scope curriculum (based largely on Piagetian theory), it can be used with any developmentally appropriate early childhood care or education

FIGURE 2.4. Example of Spectrum Observation Sheet [Adapted from Krechevsky, M. (1998). *Project Spectrum: Preschool Assessment Handbook.* New York: Teachers College Press.]

CLASSROOM MODEL OBSERVATION SHEET (Excerpt)

Child _____   Observer _____

Age _____   Date _____

1. Please show me where you spend *most of your time* playing in the classroom.

       Is that your favorite activity? Why?

       What if that place were already full of children—show me where you would go.

2. Here are some pictures of the different games that you played with _____.

       Which one do you think you were the best at?

       Why?

       Which one was hardest for you to do?

       Why?

       Which one of the games was your favorite?

3. Let's put other children where they like to play . . . show me someone in your class who *always* plays at:

       Blocks _____

       Dramatic Play _____

       Art _____

       Water Table _____

       Writing Table _____

At this point, ask child to help you return figures to magnet board before asking next question.

FIGURE 2.5. Example of Work Sampling System Developmental Guidelines [Adapted from Marsden, D., et al. (1994). *Preschool–4 Developmental Guidelines* (3rd ed.). Ann Arbor, MI: Rebus Planning Associates.]

I   PERSONAL AND SOCIAL DEVELOPMENT (Excerpts)

B   Self control

1. Follows classroom rules and routines.

Four-year-olds find established routines very comforting. They feel safer and better able to participate when rules are clear and followed consistently. They show their acceptance and understanding of rules and routines by

• knowing they have to wait until someone leaves the water table when the rule is "only four at a time";
• clearing off their place at the snack table by taking their cup to the designated place and throwing away their napkins and leftovers without frequent reminders;
• holding hands (or hanging onto a rope) when crossing a street that has no traffic light or crossing guard;
• washing hands before snack;
• removing a finished painting from the easel and knowing where to hang it to dry;
• turning off the tape recorder after listening to a story;
• knowing to go to the circle area after clean-up.

2. Uses classroom materials purposefully and respectfully.

In school, children are encouraged to take care of the materials they are using and to keep the classroom in order. Ways that children show responsibility for materials include

• helping to clean up by sweeping around the sand table;
• putting blocks away in designated spots;
• looking at books carefully; and then putting them back on the shelf when finished;
• handling objects on the Discovery Table with care
• exploring the teacher's guitar gently, thoughtfully, and with care.

3. Manages transitions.

Four-year-olds find established routines very comforting, and changing routines or doing things differently quite upsetting. Examples of managing transitions include:

• separating from a parent (or caregiver) at the door with growing ease;
• putting away a choice time activity when the clean-up signal is given;
• accepting transitions with little or no protest;
• helping the teacher give transition signals;
• putting something away ahead of schedule because a visitor has come to lead a special group time.

FIGURE 2.6. High/Scope Assessment Categories [Adapted from High/Scope Child Educational Research Foundation. (1992). *Child Observation Record for Ages 2-1/2–6.* Ypsilanti, MI: High/Scope Press.]

I.	**Initiative**	O.	Imitating movements to a steady beat
A.	Expressing choices		
B.	Solving problems	P.	Following music and movement directions
C.	Engaging in complex play		
D.	Cooperating in program routines	**V.**	**Language and Literacy**
		Q.	Understanding speech
II.	**Social Relations**	R.	Speaking
E.	Relating to adults	S.	Showing interest in reading activities
F.	Relating to other children		
G.	Making friends with other children	T.	Demonstrating knowledge about books
H.	Engaging in social problem solving	U.	Beginning reading
		V.	Beginning writing
I.	Understanding and expressing feelings		
		VI.	**Logic and Mathematics**
		W.	Sorting
III.	**Creative Representation**	X.	Using the words *not, some,* and *all*
J.	Making and building		
K.	Drawing and painting	Y.	Arranging materials in graduated order
L.	Pretending		
		Z.	Using comparison words
IV.	**Music and Movement**	AA.	Comparing numbers of objects
M.	Exhibiting body coordination	BB.	Counting objects
		CC.	Describing spatial relations
N.	Exhibiting manual coordination	DD.	Describing sequence and time

program. The COR looks at six developmental categories: initiative, social relations, creative representation, music and movement, language and literacy, and logic and mathematics.[5] These categories are intended to reflect broad aspects of children's cognitive, social-emotional, and physical development (see Figure 2.6). They correspond to key dimensions of child development identified by the National Association for the Education of Young Children (Bredekamp & Rosegrant, 1993).

Teachers using the COR system make daily observations of the children as they go about their work and play. These anecdotal observations are recorded on note cards or in a similar format, and provide the data for filling out a COR report several times a year. Like the WSS (and unlike Spectrum), the COR looks at children's general developmental status, rather than emphasizing distinctive individual strengths (see Figure 2.7). Correlations of COR ratings with scores on the McCarthy Scales of Children's Abilities (McCarthy, 1972) range from .27 to .66 (High/Scope, 1992).

Spectrum should be seen as complementary to, rather than competing with or substituting for, the COR or the WSS. Some of the differences between the three systems grow out of the original status of each initiative: Spectrum was primarily a research project designed to apply a more pluralistic and contextualized view of intelligence to the classroom; the COR was originally intended to accompany the Piagetian-based High/Scope curriculum; and WSS was developed to provide a performance-assessment alternative in a system dominated by standardized achievement tests. All three approaches include some form of narrative report and recommend collecting samples of children's work over time. Although they all emphasize the importance of observation, the WSS and COR provide a more formalized structure and set of guidelines for systematizing and documenting teachers' day-to-day observations. Also, both the WSS and COR offer professional development programs for teachers, an endeavor that Project Zero is just beginning to explore.

DISTINCTIVE FEATURES OF THE SPECTRUM APPROACH

In the years since the project's infancy, we have applied the Spectrum approach in a number of different settings. Members of our research staff have returned to classrooms and schools as teachers and administrators. Through these experiences, and experiences reported to us by educators around the country, we have learned a great deal about the features that distinguish Spectrum's approach to curriculum and assessment. We will summarize these features in the pages that follow.

- *Spectrum changes what people think of as "intelligence."*

Spectrum addresses the cognitive and intellectual aspects of activities that people do not typically think of as involving cognitive problem solving. Many of us do not usually think of moving expressively or creating a sculpture or caring for a friend as involving "intelligence" per se. Indeed, many teachers initially are uncomfortable when asked to assess children's movement ideas or artwork or interactive styles. But Spectrum challenges us to reexamine our beliefs. It calls into question our assumptions about what types of work are worth assessing and forces us to reconsider the beliefs and values that underlie our comfort in assessing only linguistic and logical-mathematical development.

FIGURE 2.7. Example of High/Scope Assessment Guidelines [Adapted from High/Scope Educational Research Foundation. (1992). *Child Observation Record for Ages 2-1/2–6.* Ypsilanti, MI: High/Scope Press.]

(Based on observations of the child during normal program activities, check off on each item the highest level of the child's typical behavior.)

II. Social Relations (Excerpts)

F. Relating to other children.

	Time 1	Time 2	Time 3
Child does not yet play with other children. (1)	___	___	___
Child responds when other children initiate interactions. (2)	___	___	___
Child initiates interactions. (3)	___	___	___
Child sustains interactions with other children. (4)	___	___	___
Child works on complex projects with other children (shares labor, follows rules). (5)	___	___	___

Notes

G. Making friends with other children.

Child does not yet identify classmates by name. (1)	___	___	___
Child identifies some of the children by name and occasionally talks about them. (2)	___	___	___
Child identifies a classmate as a friend. (3)	___	___	___
Child is identified by a classmate as a friend. (4)	___	___	___
Child appears to receive social support from a friend and shows loyalty to the friend. (5)	___	___	___

Notes

As noted earlier, one of the key features of the Spectrum approach is that it is grounded in theory. If what we value is what we assess, Spectrum provides a theoretical framework for modifying our assessment approach. Although Spectrum is not trying to cover *all* of child development, it does attempt to tap many different areas of cognition. Multiple intelligences theory specifically aims to expand the kinds of abilities and activities that can be considered "cognitive."

In many cases, helping teachers redefine intelligence is only the first step. Parents, too, may undervalue their children's abilities in "nonacademic" areas. When Janet Stork left Spectrum to become director of an early childhood program, she found the theoretical framework gave her a way of talking with parents about their children's strengths. In the case of one student, Sam, she helped the parents see their child's difficulty with language acquisition in the context of all his interests and abilities. After several conferences, they were able to appreciate that his abilities to build elaborate structures with blocks and to understand mechanical objects reflected intelligences that were worthy of recognition and development.

Spectrum is a way of looking at children and their work. Many good teachers are already aware of the dimensions that Spectrum addresses, but lack a formal system for articulating the ideas or applying them to their classrooms. Spectrum provides a framework for assessing cognitive abilities in context. The assessments can illuminate the special qualities of children's minds by helping generate hypotheses about where their strengths may lie. If teachers are mystified by a child who is unable to find a niche, or curious about a child's ability in a particular domain, they can pull out a Spectrum activity and conduct a more in-depth assessment. They then may use their findings to reshape the classroom curriculum, for example by giving children multiple ways in which to engage in a content area, using strengths as a "hook" or "bridge" to areas of difficulty, or collaborating more productively with music, art, or physical education specialists.

The Spectrum assessments provide a framework for fine-grained and domain-specific observations. Once teachers become accustomed to looking for children's strengths, they may find them in unexpected areas. Special education teacher Peg Daugherty, who had received Spectrum training along with colleagues at her Long Island primary school, found this to be the case with Zoe, a shy, tiny first-grader who was 10 months younger than her classmates (Daugherty, personal communication, 1996). During a 2-month unit on birds, Zoe revealed that she had an uncanny ability to imitate the sound of a bird singing. Her classroom teacher gave her the opportunity to duplicate many different birdcalls, an experience that gained her a newfound respect from peers and elevated her status in the classroom. Trying to build upon Zoe's sensitivity to cadence and sound, her teachers selected rhymes and poems as a way to engage her in reading.

Spectrum offers multiple entry points into the curriculum. The Spectrum assessments and framework lend breadth to the classroom. A Spectrum environment includes a broad range of activities and materials that encourage exploration across and within domains. Instead of letting specialists alone address subject areas such as music and movement, teachers build them into their classroom activity centers. Musical instruments and recordings and physical education equipment such as balance beams are more likely to be incorporated into a Spectrum environment than into a traditional one. Teachers also provide a greater range of follow-up activities and choices for projects.

In one primary school influenced by Spectrum, a kindergarten teacher, for the first time, incorporated music and movement skills into her whole-class instruction. After the group lesson, instead of conducting the same follow-up activities with the whole class, she began offering a choice of problem-solving activities designed to build on children's strengths (Kornhaber & Krechevsky, 1995).

In another school, former Spectrum researcher Miriam Raider-Roth gave 8-year-old Jose the Storyboard Activity (a storytelling activity using a board or box outfitted with figures and a setting) in an effort to figure out how to help him learn to write and read. Jose proceeded to tell a complicated story, manipulating the small figures and props on the storyboard (Raider-Roth, personal communication, 1994). When Raider-Roth realized that Jose needed to be around letters physically, she stretched her curriculum to enable him to finger paint letters, form letters with his body, and dance out stories. Through a combination of these activities, a literature-rich program, and structured phonics tutoring, Jose eventually learned to read.

Spectrum emphasizes curricular content. In addition to helping to ensure *breadth*, Spectrum also encourages *depth*. Spectrum brings a foundation in real-world disciplines to the early childhood curriculum. It does not try to push the later curriculum of the elementary years downward nor offer mere "fun and games." Rather than preparing children in preliteracy or numeracy skills, Spectrum stimulates interest in making discoveries, constructing meaning, creating notations—an approach that can be important for subsequent success in school as well as in the workplace.

Spectrum's domain-specific activities also provide a more in-depth look at children in particular areas. For instance, in the movement do-main, beyond considering the broad stages of Eric's or Kira's physical de-velopment (for example, whether they learned how to skip or balance on one foot), we also looked at their abilities to invent novel movement ideas, to evoke a mood through movement, or to complete an obstacle course with agility and speed. The Spectrum assessments have a strong content bias. But rather than reflecting traditional curriculum, the content is grounded in domain activities drawn from the nonuniversal regions of Feldman's developmental continuum.

This content bias, unusual at the preschool level, could have impli-cations for teacher education, hiring, team-teaching, and community participation. Most teacher preparation programs devote little effort to honing domain-specific observation skills outside of language and math. Rather than looking for the broadly trained generalist, a program director might hire teachers who bring expertise in a particular domain. These teachers might then team-teach with colleagues who have complementary areas of expertise or with music, art, or physical education specialists. Par-ents or mentors from the community also could be brought in to serve as role models and share different kinds of expertise. Finally, tapping com-munity resources—for example, by visiting museums and nature centers or inviting artists into the classroom—could help augment the curriculum and offer different ways to nurture children's strengths.

Spectrum emphasizes children's strengths. Unlike so many deficit-oriented forms of assessment, Spectrum emphasizes identifying and celebrating children's strengths. The framework serves as a constant reminder not to lose sight of a child's strengths in the pursuit of other educational goals. It does not assume that all children can or should develop strengths in every area assessed. Not every child will become expert in taking apart and reas-sembling mechanical objects or in completing the obstacle course. But the framework does imply that all children will have a strength in at least one content area either relative to themselves or to their age group.

Spectrum does not emphasize strengths in an abstract way. Although feeling good about oneself is an important prerequisite for learning, Americans in particular sometimes err on the side of overpraising in the absence of meaningful achievement (Damon, 1995). An approach such as Spectrum contributes substance to the "let's improve our self-esteem" rhetoric. The assessment framework provides a wide variety of areas in which meaningful problem solving and work can take place. Thus, chil-dren can feel good about themselves on the basis of specific achievements and a realistic sense of their own abilities.

In Chapter 3 we will explore the various ways that teachers can use information about children's strengths to enhance their students' learning and classroom participation. Nurturing children's strengths can include giving children opportunities to generate their own ideas; to share their ideas, products, and performances with others; and to reflect on their work and play. With older children, teachers sometimes choose to teach the theory and terminology of multiple intelligences in order to give students, parents, and new teachers a vocabulary for thinking about intelligence as more than a single dimension (Kornhaber & Krechevsky, 1995). If children see that every classmate brings a distinctive set of strengths to a learning or problem-solving situation, and that no child performs better or worse than everyone else in *all* content areas, then their respect for their peers is likely to increase. A number of schools trying to implement MI theory now are reporting that children treat one another with more respect and exhibit fewer behavior problems (Kornhaber, personal communication, 1998).

Spectrum gives teachers and students additional languages for learning. For the reasons we just discussed, Jo Gusman, now a faculty member at California State University at Sacramento, calls MI theory "the great equalizer. . . . When a teacher is mindful of all seven intelligences, it changes the status of children in the classroom." Today, Gusman trains teachers to use an MI approach to help non-English-speaking children participate more fully in school. Incorporating music, art, movement, and other symbol systems into each lesson not only helps non-English-speaking students learn and succeed, says Gusman, it helps the English-speakers too.

Gusman recalls her first week teaching kindergarten at the Newcomers School in Sacramento, a school that for about 15 years served refugees from Southeast Asia. Gusman, who speaks Spanish, was assigned 35 children who spoke 12 different languages that she could not understand. Gusman went home each day in tears. Then, she noticed how much the children enjoyed one of her records, *Annie*, and decided that the children would perform the play. She taught the children each song, one sentence at a time. They listened to the music, drew pictures of the story, and acted out the plot, learning to read and understand each line word by word. By December, the children not only performed the play—they also could converse with a reporter in English.

Spectrum changes ideas about which children should be considered "gifted and talented." Individuals working in the gifted and talented field have had a somewhat more ambivalent reaction to Spectrum. If every child has a strength in some area, then programs that target a specialized few may not be as easily justifiable. However, a number of gifted and talented programs have drawn on the Spectrum work to broaden their definition of giftedness. Directors and teachers in these programs modified the Spectrum assessment activities for use with children who typically are underrepresented in these programs—for example, children who have limited English proficiency, are developmentally delayed, or come from economically disadvantaged homes. In Chapter 6, we will examine the way one of these programs worked at a suburban preschool-through-Grade-2 public school.

CONCLUDING NOTE

In this chapter, we have described the efforts of a small team of researchers in search of a new mode of assessment. We placed the Spectrum approach in the context of other models of curriculum and assessment in early childhood. Finally, we distilled some of the defining features that make up the Spectrum framework and philosophy. We have been surprised and delighted by the positive way in which educators around the country have responded to our ideas. The Spectrum approach offers a way to transcend the sometimes warring positions of early education as a time for children either to develop academic skills and "get a leg up on the competition" or to enjoy themselves and revel in free exploration.

But a few cautionary notes are in order. First, at the risk of repeating ourselves, it is important to keep in mind that Spectrum is not a curriculum, nor a comprehensive approach to early childhood education, nor even a way to organize a classroom. It is an approach to understanding different areas of cognition—a way to think rather than something to adopt. With a Spectrum lens, we can go into any classroom or school and examine and assess what is or could be going on.

Second, any assessment of children should rely on more than one measure. The Spectrum activities yield information that should be considered in the context of everything else a teacher knows about a child. The approach should not be used to provide another set of labels for children or for premature tracking into narrow educational paths. It is intended to expand, rather than funnel or constrain, options and opportunities.

Finally, Spectrum does not tell teachers or schools what it is they should teach. Educators still must grapple with hard questions about what skills and ideas they value, and what they want children to learn. Once these questions are answered, the Spectrum approach can be a valuable tool for working on a wide range of educational goals. It can be used to give children experience in multiple domains or it can be used to shore up ability in selected content areas. A community may decide that language and social skills are important societal goals and so emphasize linguistic and interpersonal content, or it may decide to nurture all abilities equally. What is most important is that the decisions are based on an open discussion about educational goals and values.

ONCE WE HAD developed a framework for identifying and assessing relative strengths in preschool children, we were ready to explore more fully Spectrum's educational implications. Could a Spectrum approach work in a large public school? Could it improve school-age children's academic performance and, if so, by what measures? Could it capture and engage the attention of children considered at risk for school failure? The next chapter addresses these and other questions in greater detail.

NOTES

1. "Kira" is not her real name; the names of all the children mentioned in this book have been changed.

2. Many other researchers joined the team over the years, including the other coauthors of this volume, Julie Viens and Jie-Qi Chen.

3. The Early Symbolization Project was a longitudinal study that looked at the development of representational capacities in children.

4. It is interesting to note that Adams found moderate correlations between children's scores on several different pairs of activities, indicating that the cognitive abilities tested, though not unitary, may not be completely independent of one another either.

5. The original High/Scope record-keeping system had divided logic and mathematics into five areas: classification, seriation, number, space, and time.

REFERENCES

Adams, M. L. (1993). *An empirical investigation of domain-specific theories of preschool children's cognitive abilities. Unpublished doctoral dissertation.* Medford, MA: Tufts University.

Bereiter, C., & Engelmann, S. (1966). *Teaching disadvantaged children in the preschool.* Englewood Cliffs, NJ: Prentice Hall.

Bredekamp, S., & Rosegrant, T. (1993). *Researching potentials: Appropriate curriculum and assessment for young children, Vol. 1.* Washington, DC: NAEYC.

Damon, W. (1995). *Greater expectations: Overcoming the culture of indulgence in America's homes and schools.* New York: Free Press.

Edwards, C., Gandini, L., & Forman, G. (1993). *The hundred languages of children.* Norwood, NJ: Ablex.

Feinburg, S., & Mindess, M. (1994). *Eliciting children's full potential.* Belmont, CA: Brooks/Cole.

Feldman, D. H. (1991). *Nature's gambit.* New York: Basic Books. (Original work published 1986).

Gardner, H., & Hatch, T. (1989). Multiple intelligences go to school: Educational implications of the theory of multiple intelligences. *Educational Researcher, 18* (8), 4–10.

Gardner, H., Hatch, T., & Torff, B. (1997). A third perspective: The symbol systems approach. In R. Sternberg & E. Grigorenko (Eds.), *Intelligence, heredity, and environment* (pp. 243–268). New York: Cambridge University Press.

Greenberg, P. (1990). Why not academic preschool? *Young Children, 45*(2), 70–80.

High/Scope Educational Research Foundation (1992). *High/Scope Child Observation Record.* Ypsilanti, MI: High/Scope Press.

Katz, L., & Chard, S. (1989). *Engaging children's minds: The project approach.* Norwood, NJ: Ablex.

Kornhaber, M., & Krechevsky, M. (1995). Expanding definitions of teaching and learning: Notes from the MI underground. In P. Cookson & B. Schneider (Eds.), *Transforming schools* (pp. 181–208). New York: Garland.

Krechevsky, M. (1998). *Project Spectrum: Preschool assessment handbook.* New York: Teachers College Press.

Krechevsky, M., & Gardner, H. (1990). The emergence and nurturance of multiple intelligences: The Project Spectrum approach. In M. J. A. Howe (Ed.), *Encouraging the development of exceptional skills and talents* (pp. 222–245). Leicester, UK: British Psychological Society.

Marsden, D., Meisels, S. J., Jablon, J., & Dichtelmiller, M. (1994). *Preschool–4 Developmental Guidelines* (3rd ed). Ann Arbor, MI: Rebus Planning Associates.

McCarthy, D. A. (1972). *McCarthy's Scales of Children's Abilities.* New York: Psychological Corporation.

Meisels, S. J. (1993). Remaking classroom assessment with the Work Sampling System. *Young Children, 48*(5), 34–40.

Meisels, S. J., Jablon, J., Marsden, D., Dichtelmiller, M., Dorfman, A., & Steele, D. (1994). *The Work Sampling System: An overview.* Ann Arbor, MI: Rebus Planning Associates.

Meisels, S. J., Liaw, F. R., & Nelson, R. F. (1995). The Work Sampling System: Reliability and validity of a performance assessment for young children. *Early Childhood Research Quarterly, 10,* 277–296.

Montessori, M. (1964). *The Montessori method.* New York: Schocken Books.

Rauscher, F. H., Shaw, G. L., Levine, L. J., Wright, E. L., Dennis, W. R., & Newcomb, R. L. (1997). Music training causes long-term enhancement of preschool children's spatial-temporal reasoning. *Neurological Research, 19,* 2–8.

Shapiro, E., & Biber, B. (1972). The education of young children: A developmental interaction approach. *Teachers College Record, 74,* 55–79.

CHAPTER 3

SPECTRUM LEARNING CENTERS
FOR AT-RISK LEARNERS

One afternoon in early October 1990, a group of Spectrum researchers gathered with four first-grade teachers at an elementary school in Somerville, Massachusetts. Located about three miles northwest of Boston, Somerville is an economically and ethnically mixed community with a median household income somewhat below the state average. The four teachers, Mrs. Wright, Mrs. Davidson, Mrs. McCarthy, and Mrs. Paivio,[1] came from three different Somerville schools and were veteran teachers, with experience ranging from 9 to 23 years. Three of the teachers had master's degrees in education, and all four had volunteered to participate in the project. The purpose of this meeting was to help researchers and teachers learn more about each other and about the students in each of the classrooms.

It was a typical New England autumn day—warm and pleasant, with blue sky and bright sunshine. However, as we listened to teachers express their concerns for their students, we felt a slight chill in the air, as if the sky had turned gray and cloudy.

Mrs. Wright spoke first. "This year I have a number of students who, I think, will have a lot of trouble with their schoolwork. Let me give you an example. Bob is a kindergarten repeater, and still he knows almost nothing about *everything*," she said. "I've watched him closely since the beginning of the school year; he has minimal concentration and is so distractible. I mean he can't really begin a worksheet without a lot of encouragement from me. And if he does get started he rarely stays with something for more than a minute. He never asks questions, even when he needs help. Unless I'm there with him, he's fidgeting or slouching at his desk. Because I've got 24 other kids to worry about, that means he seldom finishes his work."

"You're not alone," echoed Mrs. McCarthy. "I have 25 students this year and at least 6 of them are like your Bob. Of these 25 students, most receive free lunch, 10 come from single-parent families, 7 speak languages other than English at home, at least 1 has suffered physical abuse, and 4 are now referred to the special education resource room. I wish I could help these students on an individual basis, but that isn't possible with 25 students and only one teacher in the room."

The other three teachers nodded in agreement. Mrs. Paivio added, "In my class six students are receiving remedial services this year. These kids spend a part of every morning out of the classroom. They know that they're being treated differently from their peers, and I am afraid this will affect their self-esteem."

These teachers' concerns were real. At that time, approximately two thirds of Somerville's public school students spoke English as a second language and 8 of the 10 elementary schools qualified for Chapter I federal funding for special services. Most of the teachers in this community are dedicated to improving the lives of their students, and their academic achievement in particular, but they are frustrated with the limited resources available to meet so many different needs.

Somerville is only one among many urban communities across the nation with a large number of single-parent, low-income, and new-immigrant families. Because of poverty, cultural and linguistic differences, and other factors, children from these families may begin school without the skills necessary for success in the standard academic curriculum. Furthermore, schools are not ready to address the changing backgrounds and needs of their ever more diverse populations. Although most of these children are bright and resourceful, they tend to have low academic achievement and high dropout rates. They lack self-esteem and their attitude toward school is usually poor (Hanushek, 1996; Schorr & Schorr, 1988).

Educationally disadvantaged or at-risk pupils account for almost one third of all elementary and secondary students in the United States today, and this proportion is expected to rise in the future[2] (Brodinsky & Keough, 1989; Ingels, Abraham, Karr, Spencer, & Frankel, 1992). Confronted with the rapid growth of an educationally disadvantaged population in school, all of us, as teachers and researchers, feel daunted, pressured, and challenged. Approaches that worked before may not work now; schools need to find ways to respond to the changing needs of the children they serve.

The Somerville public school system offered a fitting laboratory for this stage of our research because a majority of the children could be considered at risk for school failure. We focused our work on the first grade because the earlier the intervention, the better. Before we could propose new methods of education we needed to ask a fundamental question: Do we agree that every child can learn and wants to succeed in school and in life? If the answer was yes, then we needed to ask, Are there effective ways to approach our youngsters, particularly those who come from backgrounds that do not match our own and who not respond to our standard teaching techniques?

As Spectrum researchers, we thought about these questions in terms of the experience we had gained during the past 5 years and the issues we wished to investigate further. We realized we would face several major challenges in our effort to transform our research model into an approach suitable for public schools. First, the Spectrum approach had been used successfully to assess a wide range of skills and proclivities in 4-year-olds from a primarily European American, middle-class population. Could this approach be effective with children who were older and came from different backgrounds?

Second, in the research model, Spectrum assessment tasks typically were administered on a one-on-one basis. This technique is not practical for teachers interested in ongoing assessment in the classroom. Could we develop assessment techniques that teachers could incorporate into their daily practice, such as an informal observational checklist? How could we insure that these informal observations would provide accurate information about children's behavior and performance?

Third, assuming that we were able to identify children's distinctive profiles of abilities in the context of the classroom, how could we use this information? How could we integrate assessment, curriculum, and instruction so that children's areas of strength and interests not only were identified but also nurtured?

Last, although we believed in the value and validity of each of the multiple intelligences, we were keenly aware that academic achievement in the current school system often depends on the development of a child's linguistic and logical-mathematical abilities. If a child's strengths were identified in nontraditional domains, such as visual arts or mechanics and construction, could we use these strengths to meet other academic goals? And how could we build these bridges?

Bearing these questions in mind, we proposed three broad objectives for our work with the Somerville first-grade classrooms. These objectives were

(1) introducing children to a wide range of learning areas;
(2) identifying and supporting children's areas of strength; and
(3) utilizing children's strengths to improve overall academic performance.

We knew that we faced new challenges as we turned our attention to a more at-risk and diverse student population than we had worked with in the past. In addition, the Somerville teachers would be encountering multiple intelligences theory and the Spectrum approach for the first time. We expected difficulties and missteps. But we also hoped that Spectrum might offer an alternative approach to educating youngsters, one that would increase the likelihood of school success for those students who tend to fall between the cracks.

INTRODUCING CHILDREN TO A WIDE
RANGE OF LEARNING AREAS

In order to introduce children systematically to a wide range of intellectual areas, we adopted a learning center approach. We expanded the seven domains targeted by the Spectrum assessment instruments into eight, separating natural science from mechanics and construction because the two areas require rather different materials. Thus, the domains addressed by the Spectrum learning centers were language, math, natural science, mechanics and construction, art, social understanding, music, and movement. Each learning center was equipped with a variety of engaging materials, either commercially produced, handmade, or recycled. The music learning center, for example, might have percussion instruments, sound cylinders, a tape recorder, and audiotapes; the mechanics and construction learning center might have a wooden table, an old typewriter, and a variety of tools and gadgets including broken clocks and pencil sharpeners, plus blocks and construction toys.

The structure of the Spectrum learning centers was flexible. They could be corners, tables, or other areas of the classroom specifically set aside for carrying out domain-related activities; or they could be collections of domain-related materials available for children's use during "choice time" or more structured periods.

Upon hearing about the learning center approach, Mrs. McCarthy voiced concern. "I had learning centers in my classroom 20 years ago and the approach didn't work then," she said. "Why should I believe that it will work today?" It is true that the learning center approach was not a new concept in educational practice. In fact, Spectrum learning centers shared certain features with the learning centers used in many quality early childhood programs. These features included the use of hands-on materials and small-group activities, and participation by choice.

What distinguishes Spectrum learning centers is their foundation in multiple intelligences theory. They were designed to identify systematically and then support children's areas of strength and interest in the diverse domains. In order to develop the activities that children would perform at the learning centers, we first refined and modified eight sets of key abilities developed during the earlier Spectrum work. We defined "key abilities" as the abilities or cognitive skills that children need to perform tasks successfully in each area of knowledge. In the case of music, key abilities included music perception, production, and composition. We also identified, in greater detail, the "core components" or specific cognitive skills that typified these abilities; for example, music perception involves sensitivity to dynamics (loud and soft); sensitivity to tempo and rhythmic patterns; the ability to discriminate pitch; and the abilities to identify musical styles as well as different instruments and sounds. (For the list of key abilities, see Appendix B.)

The key abilities played an important role in both learning and assessment at the learning centers. On the one hand, we strove to present teachers and children with activities that would foster each of the key abilities. On the other hand, teachers could use the list of key abilities as observational guidelines, directing their attention to children's specific strengths and weaknesses in different domains. As a result, the Spectrum learning centers offered not only rich materials and domain-specific activities, but also a tool for guiding teachers' classroom observations as children explored the materials or engaged in the activities.

Despite the unique characteristics of the Spectrum learning center approach, we knew that the design itself would not guarantee successful implementation in the classroom. Therefore we could not answer Mrs. McCarthy's question immediately. The possibility of Spectrum learning centers working in Somerville depended on many factors, such as teachers' understanding of multiple intelligences theory and the Spectrum approach, the degree to which teachers were comfortable with the implementation of learning centers, the fit between learning centers and teachers' curriculum goals, and the extent of children's active participation in the activities. Although the Spectrum learning centers were comprised of a variety of engaging exercises and materials, they were not just a set of curriculum activities. Rather, they were the vehicle for practicing Spectrum's theory-based approach to individualized learning. Teacher understanding of and support for the theory was essential.

To familiarize teachers with the Spectrum approach, we held an intensive 2-day workshop during the summer. Before the workshop, we asked the four classroom teachers to read materials describing the Spectrum philosophy and each of the learning centers. During the workshop, David Feldman and Howard Gardner presented their thoughts on introducing the Spectrum approach into the classroom. We also invited two Somerville kindergarten teachers with whom we had worked during the 1988–89 school year. These two teachers used a Modified Spectrum Field Inventory (MSPFI) in their classrooms. MSPFI is a shortened version of the

Spectrum assessment instrument used at the Eliot-Pearson Children's School and is intended to measure diverse cognitive abilities in kindergarten and first grade rather than preschool children. They described their experiences using Spectrum assessment information for curriculum planning. Next we explained the design, nature, and structure of each learning center, and let the teachers explore the materials and try some of the activities themselves.

During the workshop, we also discussed many practical issues with the teachers, including learning center implementation strategies, management issues, and parent involvement. In addition, we talked about how teachers could use our lists of key abilities to structure their observations and identify children's areas of strength. We believe that this workshop helped make teachers comfortable with the Spectrum approach and curriculum materials and also helped hone their observational skills in each learning center area.

Immediately after the workshop, we sent each teacher a set of eight "Learning Center Activities Guides." These guides described the activities we had designed or collected for each of our eight learning centers (language, math, natural science, mechanics and construction, art, social understanding, music, and movement).[3] Each guide included a brief introduction to the domain, a description of the key abilities we had identified, a list of materials used in the learning center, and step-by-step instructions for implementing the activities. Each guide also provided several "take-home activities" that corresponded to in-class activities and were designed to involve parents in the process of discovering and nurturing their child's areas of strength.

The guides were intended to provide a structure that might help teachers implement the learning centers, not to constrain teachers' own ideas or initiatives. We hoped that our work would serve as a catalyst, making it easier for teachers to develop their own activities and projects. From the beginning, we strongly encouraged the teachers to adapt the learning center activities to their own situations and needs.

All four teachers began implementing learning centers with great enthusiasm in late September. Although they shared certain objectives, they introduced the learning centers using distinctly different methods. For example, Mrs. Wright preferred a structured approach. She opened two to four learning centers for one hour, twice a week, throughout most of the year. Taking advantage of a rather large classroom space, she set up each learning center in an area where a large group of children could gather for an introductory meeting. At that time, Mrs. Wright usually presented materials from the center and asked the children what the materials could be used for. She frequently referred to the activities guides when she explained the learning center goals and described the activities. After this introduction, Mrs. Wright often assigned the children to three or four small groups that would work on different activities either across domains or within the same domain. For example, different groups in the movement area could be playing with jump ropes, beanbags, bowling pins, and hula hoops.

Mrs. Davidson felt less comfortable using small-group activities to introduce a learning center. During the first 3 months she introduced learning centers almost exclusively through large-group activities. As children became familiar with many of the activities, the learning center time became more of a free-choice time, when a number of activities across all domains were made available. Often, individual or small groups of children worked on activities with which they had had some previous experience while Mrs. Davidson led one small group in a new activity.

The other two teachers also developed methods of implementing learning centers that reflected their own teaching styles as well as their students' needs. For example, Mrs. Paivio maintained a learning center area in the classroom that remained "open" all the time. In this way, she thought, she could invite students to engage in prolonged projects throughout the week, or ask them to work on learning center activities after they finished other classroom assignments. Mrs. McCarthy, on the other hand, scheduled specific learning center times two or three times a week. Although her class usually worked at the learning centers in the afternoon, she often introduced the activities at morning group time. She described the activities, demonstrated materials, generated rules with the children, and either assigned or had the children choose their preferred activities. Then she returned to the regular curriculum lessons for the rest of the morning. After lunch recess, children would go immediately to their assigned or chosen centers.

Between late September and late November, the teachers introduced all eight learning centers to their students. The introductory period served three purposes. It acquainted children with the procedure for choosing and carrying out activities in the learning centers without direct teacher supervision. It gave children an early opportunity to explore all the domains, particularly those of special interest. Finally, it gave teachers an initial sense of how they might best incorporate the Spectrum learning center approach into their classrooms.

Children's responses to the learning center activities were overwhelmingly positive. They expressed real pleasure with the learning centers and were excited when new ones were introduced. When we walked into the classroom we frequently heard comments such as, "Yeah, Spectrum. Awesome!" "Look, we're doing the art part of Spectrum!" "Did you hear what the teacher said? She's going to open up a new learning center today!" "Oh, goodie, Spectrum!" After the second learning center time Mrs. Wright received a special note from one of her students. It said, "Schooll is fun espeshaly wehn we do prodgex." (School is fun, especially when we do projects [Spectrum activities].)

Many children looked forward to the regular learning center times. Some teachers noticed that attendance was higher on the learning center dates. One day, a student in Mrs. Wright's class had a temperature of 102°. The teacher telephoned the student's mother to take her home. The child refused to leave, saying, "Today we're having learning center time and I don't want to miss it." In exit interviews with children, one of the questions we asked was, "What's special about Spectrum activities?" A majority of the children (71% of the total sample of 119) gave a positive response. One student said Spectrum activities were "more fun. You do art, music, mechanical, and all sorts of things." Other comments included, "They're fun and you can still learn," and "Learning centers are special because you try to do hard things but you don't have to sit at a desk with paper and pencils."

Children's descriptions were fairly accurate; Spectrum learning centers offered a variety of hands-on materials suited to different learning styles. Spectrum provided a sharp contrast to the regular classroom lessons, which often involved paper-and-pencil desk work on a single subject at a specific time. During learning center time, the children especially enjoyed experimenting with different modes of activity, such as drawing, assembling objects, and moving creatively.

At the outset of this project, we had identified the 15 children in the group at the highest risk of school failure, using five tests (two reading achievement tests, one math test, a measure of academic self-esteem, and a measure of school adjustment) and teacher evaluation of four factors (difficulty in meeting the curricular goals of kindergarten, low self-esteem, inappropriate classroom behavior, and attitudinal problems). Our observational data showed that when learning center time and regular classroom lessons were compared (MANOVA—multivariate analysis of variance), these at-risk children scored significantly higher on self-direction ($F = 3.42$, $p < .01$), positive classroom behavior ($F = 3.13$, $p < .05$), positive affect ($F = 3.52$, $p < .01$), and activity engagement ($F = 3.74$, $p < .01$) during learning center time (Chen, 1993). Teachers frequently commented that it was easy to get the children to participate in Spectrum activities but often difficult to stop them at the end of the day.

During learning center time, most of the children worked with energy and zeal on the hands-on activities. They talked with one another about their work, often using an energetic tone that rose and fell in volume throughout the period. For example, we heard the following remarks: "Hey, I jumped over! I jumped over, and the beanbag didn't fall!" during the Spectrum Obstacle Course; "Oh, oh, this doesn't work!" "Can I help you?" "No, I want to do it myself!" during a building activity in the mechanical learning center; and "Look! What have I got here? Does it look like a snake?" during a science experiment with water droplets. Although the noise sometimes frustrated teachers, the children were truly engaged; thus, they were much less disruptive and posed fewer discipline problems than during other periods of instruction.

The teachers were pleased, in general, when they saw children's enjoyment of school increase during learning center time. However, they also struggled with time commitment and other management issues, and wondered where the Spectrum activities would lead. The teachers frequently approached us with questions, such as "How can we supervise many different activities simultaneously and not be driven crazy?" "How can we stop children's work at the end of the day more effectively?" "How can we increase the power of the learning centers to help identify children's strengths or interests?" and "How can we connect children's learning center experiences with their schoolwork?"

After observing the teachers' implementation strategies and the children's positive reactions for a few months, we believed that we had accomplished our first objective—introducing children to and engaging them in a wider range of learning areas. Challenged by the teachers' questions, however, we knew that it was time to try to move forward.

IDENTIFYING AND SUPPORTING CHILDREN'S AREAS OF STRENGTH

The teachers' concerns seemed to us to focus primarily on learning center management and identifying children's strengths. These issues were intertwined. Although the second objective of our study was to help children by identifying and continually supporting their strengths, this goal could not be attained without successful implementation of the learning centers. Teachers had to feel comfortable that the learning centers were running smoothly before they could make themselves more available to help individual students. And teachers also had to feel comfortable with us before we could work together to address any problems that might arise.

Teacher and researcher collaboration is never an easy task, especially when the researchers come from a place like Harvard University. Some teachers believe that Harvard researchers have answers for everything. "What do you expect from us?" our Somerville colleagues asked. "How are we going to do this in the right way?" These questions indicated that the biggest stumbling block for teachers in using Spectrum learning centers in their classrooms might have been psychological pressure and uncertainty. So we turned the tables and asked the teachers, "What are *your* expectations?" "How could your teaching experience contribute to this research?"

In our conversations with the teachers, we tried to send the message that their experimentation and risk taking were critical to the study. We did have our research agenda, but the course we had charted was not fixed; we could always make adjustments to meet the needs of the teachers and the students. We helped the teachers recognize how much they had accomplished and told them how impressed we were by the quality of learning center implementation so far. It was they who made Spectrum learning centers alive in the classroom. Only through teamwork—the collaboration of teachers and researchers—could Spectrum's goal be realized.

We assured the teachers that they need not worry too much about the research agenda, because we recognized that organizing and directing more than 20 children as they performed activities in several different domains was an important task in itself. To better support the teachers, we concentrated on management issues and adjusted some of our research components. For example, we made our meetings more structured. From the beginning of the study we had met with the teachers weekly on a one-on-one basis as well as monthly as a group, sharing general reflections. In order to make these meetings more productive, we developed several questions we would ask each week. These questions included

- What went well this week and why?
- What do you think was difficult this week and why?
- Did a child show an interest in a particular activity or learning center? Why do you think so?
- Which learning center(s) and activities will be open next week and how will children be introduced to and experience the activities?

These questions helped teachers and researchers talk in concrete terms and focus on how to do a better job the following week. Meetings thus became more constructive and informative.

The monthly meetings gave teachers the opportunity to exchange information, share success stories, and generate management strategies together. Mrs. Davidson, for example, talked about how she used a cooperative approach during learning center time and how students turned to each other as sources of knowledge, assistance, and encouragement. Mrs.

McCarthy shared her experience in setting clear limits while still allowing children to make choices (e.g., a child may stay as long as he or she wishes in one center if the number of children in the center does not exceed the limit).

Mrs. Paivio introduced a chart she had developed to help children keep track of the learning center activities they had completed. The chart listed children's names down the side and activities, organized by domain, across the top. When a child had completed an activity she would mark the appropriate space. This chart served as an efficient record-keeping method for Mrs. Paivio and the children, who were sure to remind their teacher if they had not been chosen for a particular activity they were looking forward to. Clearly, every teacher had important ideas to share. The teachers said that the meetings helped them feel that they had accomplished something worthwhile, and that the opportunity to discuss specific strategies with their peers was most useful to their classroom practice.

Each teacher also had her own questions about or difficulties in implementing learning centers, and we tried to brainstorm solutions. For one teacher, we recommended introducing only one new learning center activity per day and having fewer centers open at a time, to make Spectrum sessions more manageable. We suggested that two teachers invite school specialists to the classrooms to help implement the learning center activities with which they felt less comfortable. And we asked the fourth teacher to allow students to make more choices during learning center time because these choices were critical for the identification of children's areas of strength.

In our earlier research at the Eliot-Pearson Children's School, we used a battery of tests to assess each child individually in all the learning center domains. For public school classrooms, we needed a less time-consuming method of identifying children's strengths. We would rely primarily on classroom observations to gather data, and with the teachers, we developed two criteria to guide us. The first was the competence that a child demonstrated in an area, evaluated in terms of the key abilities in that area (for example, numerical reasoning and logical problem solving in math, or body control and sensitivity to rhythm in movement). We posted a list of key abilities near each learning center for teachers to use while observing children's behavior and performances. The second criterion that we used for identifying children's areas of strength was the interest that a child showed in a particular area, measured by the frequency with which he or she chose that area during learning center time and the length of time that the child remained involved there.

Whenever a learning center was open in a classroom, a Spectrum researcher or graduate student would be present to observe the implementation of the center and the children's behaviors. Observational data gathered by researchers and graduate students was usually systematic and detailed, whereas observations by the classroom teachers (who were supervising their classes at the same time) were often scattered and less systematic. This drawback, however, was overcome during the weekly teacher-researcher meetings, when the two could reflect together upon the events of the past week and discuss children's demonstrated areas of strength.

Not long after we focused our attention on identifying children's strengths, we began to hear exciting stories from all four teachers. Mrs. Davidson made the following report:

> "Crystal really surprised me in the social learning center. Frankly, I always thought that Crystal was quiet and listless because you hardly hear anything from her and she seldom shows interest in anything in the class. Oh, no, no! She is completely different when she is in the social learning area—you just can't believe, when doing dress-up Crystal was constantly moving, talking, and singing! When doing puppets she was constantly giving the directions! I would have never known where her strength lies if the social learning area were not available in the classroom."

Mrs. Wright told an equally remarkable story about Bob, the child she had described at the beginning of the year as "knowing almost nothing about everything." The day she introduced the mechanics and construction learning center to the class, Bob not only knew the names of all the tools she presented, but to her great surprise also raised his hands a few times to answer the questions. Upon Mrs. Wright's request, Bob demonstrated how to use some of the tools in front of the class. When working in the mechanical area, Bob again displayed great skill and competence. For example, it took him only 5 minutes to take apart and assemble an oil pump, a challenging task for many adults.

Bob's social skills also looked quite different when he was in the mechanical area. Although he was not a troublemaker, Mrs. Wright had reported earlier, he rarely interacted with his peers. He seemed to react passively to his surroundings, and often appeared to be wandering around and fatigued. In the mechanical area, however, he offered to help two girls who were having trouble figuring out how to put together the oil pump. When his offer was rejected, he kindly suggested, "You don't have to take this apart, just open it." Later, he worked with the girls, and even requested that one girl help him complete the task. He said, "Hey, Michelle, you hold here. Then, I can put this nut on." His classmates often asked for Bob's help in the mechanical area because "he [was] so good at it."

Crystal and Bob are only two examples. In fact, in our Somerville project, we identified areas of strength for 13 of the 15 at-risk students (about 87%). These children's strengths spanned many areas, including art, mechanics and construction, social understanding, math, language, science, and movement. It is also important to note that these children demonstrated more strengths in nonacademic areas than in academic ones (six in art, three in mechanics and construction, and three in movement versus two in language and one in math).

The stories that teachers told about Bob, Crystal, and other students suggested two important conclusions. First, our observations told us that when children recognized that they were good at something, and when that skill also was recognized by the teacher and peers, the children experienced success and felt valued. When children worked in an area of strength, they not only had the chance to be effective and productive, but also to help others who were less skilled in the area. When their competence was acknowledged in the classroom, the children saw themselves as capable in the school environment, and their self-esteem was enhanced. Quantitative data that we collected supported these observations. We compared the way children worked in areas of strength to their work habits in other areas (nonstrength), and found that the children obtained significantly higher scores on all six measures we used (MANOVA test: self-direction $F = 3.98$, $p < .01$; self-confidence $F = 3.96$, $p < .01$; positive classroom behavior $F = 3.67$, $p < .01$; positive affect $F = 3.96$, $p < .01$; self-monitoring $F = 3.19$, $p < .01$; and activity engagement $F = 4.26$, $p < .010$) (Chen, 1993).

Second, reports from all the classrooms suggested that students who had trouble with some academic subjects, such as reading or math, were not necessarily inadequate in all areas. When many different learning areas were available to explore and to pursue, children could demonstrate competence and skill in a variety of areas. Equally important to the identification of children's areas of strength was continuing support. Only through a sustained effort could children's areas of strength be nurtured and developed.

The Spectrum team developed various techniques to nurture children's identified strengths. Individually, these techniques could help teachers respond to different needs and situations; together, they helped create an environment in which children's strengths were recognized and supported. For instance, to bolster children's interest in mechanics and construction, teachers could keep that area open all the time and change the materials frequently. They also could encourage the children to explore the area further, develop new projects, share their learning experience with others, and display the products on the walls of the school hallway or at an open house for parents.

Another technique for fostering a child's strength was inviting him or her to serve as activity leader in that area. The child could be asked to lead classmates to the center, serve as a resource for them, manage materials and cleanup, and help train the next leader. Mrs. Paivio often used activity leaders to help her implement the mechanical learning center because she felt that she was less knowledgeable and competent in that area than many of her students.

Informing parents about their child's areas of strength was another way in which teachers created a supportive environment. In the past, teachers had often found it hard to write positive comments on the report cards of those students who had learning difficulties or behavioral problems in school. Using the learning center information, teachers now were able to give the parents of troubled students some concrete and meaningful examples of their youngsters' intellectual strengths.

Nurturing children's strengths did not mean limiting their experience in other areas. Rather, a wide range of learning experiences enabled children to manifest and develop fully their potential, interests, abilities, and strengths. In the concluding interview we asked children whether they had learned that they were good at new kinds of things throughout the year, and 76 out of 119 students (65%) responded yes. Some children said, "I never knew I was good at so many things." One exclaimed, "I now know I could be a good artist. Mrs. Paivio said that, too."

We also noticed that when working in their interest or skill areas, the children, particularly those who had difficulty with schoolwork, often appeared transformed. Among the attributes we observed were enjoyment, happiness, enthusiasm, creativity, spontaneity, engagement, concentration, socialization, cooperation, and an apparent increase in self-confidence and self-esteem.

EXTENDING CHILDREN'S STRENGTHS TO ACADEMIC LEARNING

The story, however, does not end here. The next chapter would be even more challenging as we tried to connect the children's identified strengths to their regular schoolwork. In Bob's case, for example, was it possible for the teacher to extend Bob's mechanical strength to his academic learning? Bob was believed to be poor in both visual perception and fine motor coordination. On the Clymer-Barrett test (a school readiness test), his score in completing shapes was the lowest in the class. Among 20 shapes, he could complete only the 4 easiest ones. He also had difficulty in distinguishing between the numbers 6 and 9. Although he clearly had some visual-spatial problems in paper-and-pencil work, these problems were not at all evident when the task became a hands-on and "real-world" experience, such as construction or assembly. Bob's competence in the mechanical area revealed not only fine motor skills and visual-spatial ability, but also effective problem-solving skills. We now asked ourselves how we could transfer Bob's cognitive abilities, such as visual-spatial perception, from a nontraditional learning area to academic learning areas. More generally, how could we build children's strengths (such as Bob's strength in working with tools) into other areas of learning, particularly those areas central to success in school?

This question reflected a major concern of all of the teachers. On one hand, they recognized the overall impact of the Spectrum learning centers on classroom atmosphere and students' attitudes toward school. Again and again they acknowledged that the Spectrum activities gave the children much enjoyment and helped make the school year a very happy one. On the other hand, they felt a tension between the demands of the regular school curriculum and Spectrum's agenda. The teachers said that it took a great deal of time to prepare and implement the Spectrum learning centers. Given the difficulties that their students were having in traditional academic areas, they wondered whether available resources should be focused directly on these problems.

We were getting to the heart of an important issue—what is the most effective way to help struggling children master basic skills and improve academic performance? Traditional intervention programs often focus on a child's weaknesses in reading and math and tend to emphasize lower level basic skills, such as arithmetic operations and procedures in mathematics and decoding skills in reading. The instructional approach typically employed is drill and practice, including workbook sheets that require children to practice skills divorced from context and application. Although we could see that some students might benefit from this type of teaching strategy, others might be bored and frustrated or lack the motivation needed to do the work. These latter students might be more responsive to a different approach, one that embedded basic skills in meaningful activities and built upon their own interests and strengths.

We called this concept "bridging," and testing it was the third objective of our study. We defined bridging as using children's experiences in their areas of strength as pathways into other learning areas and academic performances. In practice, however, we had little experience with the bridging process. We needed to figure out the mechanisms, such as how teachers could link children's strengths to academic learning during learning center time; how bridges could be built to specific curriculum lessons; how learning takes place in the bridging process; and what factors other than strengths can influence the bridging process. We devoted several of our teacher-researcher meetings to answering these questions and developing strategies for putting the concept of bridging into practice.

Through our discussions we came to realize that the bridging process probably has two layers: whole group and individualized. On the classroom level, teachers could bridge their students' strengths to other areas of learning by means of peer interactions, group activities, and a project-centered approach. General intervention could be followed up with specific help for individuals. At this individualized level, a child's strengths and weaknesses would be identified through classroom observation. Educational "treatments" or activities then could be tailored to the child's strengths, working styles, personality, and other social characteristics. Obviously, any intervention plan would require ongoing adjustment to account for progress and other changes in the child's needs.

This framework helped direct our efforts. We developed several strategies for bridging on the classroom level. First, we asked teachers to consider incorporating learning center ideas, materials, and activities into their math or language arts curricula. Teachers found that many learning center activities could be used to enhance children's acquisition of basic reading and math skills. For example, some teachers asked their students to send letters and postcards to friends or relatives via the classroom mailbox. They found that the students produced a greater quantity and higher quality of writing than for other assignments, an improvement they attributed to the meaningfulness of the letter-writing activity. With a little creativity, teachers could use materials from virtually any of the learning centers to reinforce reading and math skills. In the mechanics and construction area, children could label tools or write their names by hammering nails into a piece of wood. In the science learning center, they could sort, graph, or count the sink-and-float materials. In the social learning center, children could use the puppet theater to read a book or tell stories to an audience of classmates.

Mrs. Davidson came up with the idea for another bridging strategy for the whole class, which we called the "project approach." She infused Spectrum ideas and activities into her regular curriculum, which was built around themes and projects. When she was planning a unit on outer space, she found it helpful to use the concept of multiple intelligences as the framework for organizing her projects. With the assistance of a Spectrum researcher, Mrs. Davidson adapted learning center activities from a variety of domains to advance her instructional goals. For example, she asked children to interview classmates on various topics in astronomy, and then categorize and graph their responses. This exercise was adapted from a Spectrum social learning center activity called Class Census. She also adapted a language activity called "Storyboard," giving students different props and materials related to outer space that could be used to tell, draw, dictate, or write stories. As children exercised different intelligences, learning became meaningful, connected, and fun. In addition, children's understanding of scientific concepts became deeper and broader. Furthermore, the various intelligences were used to gain access to central themes, and thus became a means of learning rather than goals in and of themselves.

We also discovered the importance of "cognitive apprenticeship" in enhancing the bridging process. As we observed children's behavior and performance during learning center time, we found that engaging materials could invite children's participation in activities, but did not automatically enable them to develop skills. Spectrum activities were far more than games—they embraced many cognitive and basic skills that could not easily be grasped by children without a teacher's scaffolding and guidance.

Teachers needed to act as coaches and facilitators to guide and challenge students' learning and thinking. We encouraged the teachers to ask children thought-provoking questions and to pose problems, suggest different hypotheses, and urge children to test these hypotheses in a variety of ways. We were confident that even if critical-thinking capabilities did not directly relate to the mastery of basic skills, they would have value in the children's learning process.

At the individualized level, we envisioned a number of different ways that bridging could work. Confidence building might be one method of linking strengths to other intellectual areas. More specifically, when a child discovers an area of strength, enjoys exploring it, and feels good about him- or herself, the experience of being successful could give the child the confidence to enter more demanding domains. The learning style particular to the child's area of strength could be another possible vehicle for engaging the child in an area of challenge. For example, putting numbers to music might encourage an auditory learner to play number games. A third possibility would be to use the content of a child's areas of strength to engage him or her in other areas. For example, a child with mechanical interests and abilities could be asked to read and write about machines. Finally, we assumed that some structural component of an area of strength might be relevant to performance in another area. For example, a child sensitive to the rhythmic aspect of music might also respond to rhythmic aspects of language or movement.

In theory, we had isolated different ways of bridging. In practice, however, we knew that a child's learning is a complex process; it involves the interactions and combinations of many factors. Accordingly, we developed a diagnostic/prescriptive model to help teachers with the bridging process. In this model, teachers would list a child's strengths in terms of learning center domains. They then would list the child's weaknesses, asking themselves the question, "What would I like the child to be able to do that he or she is not doing now?" Teachers would choose one weakness on which to concentrate and write down the goal they wished to attain. They also might discuss the goal with the child to make him or her a partner in the bridging process. Next, teachers would brainstorm bridging activities that might lead from the child's areas of strength toward the targeted goal.

At our teacher-researcher meetings, we began to select those children who appeared to need the most help and to use the diagnostic/prescriptive model to brainstorm various bridging activities. For example, Crystal had demonstrated strength in the social learning area. Her teacher wondered if this strength could be extended to improve such math skills as addition and subtraction. She worked with a Spectrum researcher to develop several bridging activities. In one of these projects, Crystal surveyed her classmates on a question, tallied the responses, and noted the differences between various groups (girls and boys, different eye colors, different birthdays).

We also explored various ways of bridging Bob's mechanical strength to the reading and writing curriculum. Our ideas included asking Bob to help label all the tools in the classroom, make a list of the tools, and supervise borrowing; training him to be the mechanical learning center leader and encouraging him to help other children solve the mechanics and construction problems; asking him to draw and write about his experience working with tools and to share this work with classmates during learning center reflection time; involving him in real mechanical activities in the classroom such as fixing the easels; communicating with his resource room teacher about Bob's strengths, needs, and learning styles; and reporting to his parents about his competence in the mechanical area and asking their help in applying his strength to academic learning.

As the teachers invested more of their energy in bridging, we began to see results. Overall, Spectrum learning centers had a productive and industrious tone that spring. Children explored many materials and created a variety of pieces—including clay sculptures, finger puppets, watercolor paintings, and book-related storyboards—that displayed imagination, expressiveness, and a high level of detail. They also completed an elaborate water pollution project with activities from several different domains.

Several teachers also made impressive strides in helping individual children. One of these successes involved Tom, a child who had great difficulty in the language arts areas of the curriculum. His teacher, Mrs. McCarthy, had already discovered that Tom displayed great strength in the mechanics and construction learning center in terms of his skill level as well as his evolving leadership role. To connect language skills with Tom's love for mechanical tasks, Mrs. McCarthy suggested that he create a "tool dictionary," or manual, for the mechanical learning center.

At the beginning of the project, Tom drew some tools and dictated brief "definitions" to Mrs. McCarthy. He then labeled each tool himself. Gradually, his dictation became longer and more detailed and his language became more poetic. "Pliers are used to cut wires," he composed. "Screwdrivers screw in screws into wood." As his confidence in his descriptions grew, Tom began to switch his focus from drawing and dictating to writing, first with, and later without, the teacher's assistance. His growth seemed to illustrate Vygotsky's concept of a "zone of proximal development," which describes the importance of adult assistance in helping children achieve a higher level of performance than when they work independently (Vygotsky, 1934/1986). Mrs. McCarthy commented at this point that Tom read the journal back to her every day. Although she knew he was reciting it from memory, she also knew that he felt successful with the bridging experience.

Mrs. McCarthy pointed out that the tool dictionary was a breakthrough for both Tom and for herself. For Tom, the writing project was the first task outside the learning center in which he was self-directed and self-motivated. Mrs. McCarthy began to feel that the energy she invested in the learning centers was "paying off," in terms of both understanding her students and planning her curriculum.

So she decided to develop bridging activities for Brad, a student who demonstrated strength in the social area but also had great difficulty in reading and writing. Mrs. McCarthy asked him to pick a child each day and either draw or dictate one nice thing about that child. Because Brad tended to concentrate on a task better when working with other children, Mrs. McCarthy often would assign a child who had finished his or her work early to be a "scribe" for Brad. Mrs. McCarthy also asked Brad to use the classroom model, and his sensitive observations of the class, to make up stories. A student teacher helped tape and transcribe one of the stories, which Brad illustrated and read to his teachers and his peers.

Mrs. McCarthy's success stories demonstrated the feasibility of bridging not only as a strategy for helping individual children, but also as a vehicle for teacher development. Recall that at the beginning of the year, all of the teachers questioned the learning center approach. Now that they had experienced the power of this approach to advance children's learning and development, they were thinking about alternatives to their standard curriculum. At the beginning of the year, the teachers' major concern was how poorly their students were prepared for formal learning. Now they were interested in discovering children's areas of strength and revamping their lesson plans to build upon children's abilities. As Mrs. Davidson pointed out, "I must say that this is the year of big growth for my students as well as for myself. I have learned so much and changed so much. I am now thinking of curriculum in much broader domains of learning. When I was planning the curriculum, I often thought of children's areas of strength and how to foster these strengths. Spectrum has clearly influenced my teaching and my perspective on children."

REFLECTING UPON THE YEAR

Time flew. It was an afternoon in early June 1991, when the Spectrum collaboration team, teachers and researchers, once again were gathered together. This time, we were saying good-byes filled with many different emotions. We felt regret, for a one-year experiment was too short to make a lasting, profound impact on students' academic achievement. For example, we did not see significant gains in achievement test scores in the four Spectrum classrooms, in part because of the short length of the intervention. It has been well documented that it requires a much longer period than one year to observe the impact of attitudinal and behavioral changes (which were achieved through our interventions) on the mastery of basic skills (Comer, 1988; Hanushek, 1996). But we also felt pride, for we all had learned a great deal during this period and benefited from our collaboration with each other.

At last we were able to answer some of the questions we had raised at the beginning of the year. From classroom experiences and observations, as well as evaluation of and interviews with the students, we concluded that the Spectrum approach had been effective in identifying and supporting the strengths of the Somerville first graders who had participated in the project.

In our Somerville work, Spectrum learning centers had made it possible to introduce children to many different areas of learning and many different methods of demonstrating their competence. The activities also were fun, and thus seemed to foster an enjoyment of school. Although we chose to implement eight learning centers in a systematic way, there are many other ways in which the Spectrum approach could be brought into the classroom. Teachers, for example, could incorporate language and math learning center activities into their standard curriculum lessons; use learning center activities from a variety of domains in planning a project-based unit; use learning center activities to support other instructional practices, such as whole language, cooperative learning, or tutoring; or invent many different approaches of their own.

Our experience also showed that the Spectrum approach holds special promise for children from disadvantaged backgrounds. Although many children at risk for school failure may exhibit weaknesses in reading or math, our Somerville work supported our belief that these children are bright, capable, and have many cognitive strengths that are overlooked in more traditional educational programs. The many cases we described, in this and in earlier chapters, reveal that if these children are given the opportunity to work in their areas of strength, they can acquire new skills and appear more competent to themselves and to others. Drawing attention to and nurturing at-risk children's areas of strength offers a promising alternative to the all too typical characterization of this population as deficient.

In fact, one of Project Spectrum's long-term goals is to reduce the need for special services such as classroom "pull-out" by providing classroom-based support and enhancing the teacher's ability to reach at-risk children in the regular first grade classroom. This approach, however, is not recommended in all cases. For example, the Spectrum approach may not be appropriate for children who have severe emotional, physical, or learning problems. Recognition of the limits of the approach is as important to its successful implementation as awareness of its possibilities.

If the Spectrum approach can indeed be used to improve academic performance, our teacher-researcher team concluded, a key element will be bridging. Our experience showed us that successful bridging is a very time-consuming process, requiring great effort and wisdom to plan and carry out, and demanding many one-on-one interactions between the teacher and the child. In our one-year study, we were not able to show measurable effects of the bridging process on classroom academic achievement as a whole. However, we did see positive changes in classroom behaviors and cases in which bridging seemed to have a profound effect on the individual child.

Moreover, we believe that the bridging process merits further investigation as an alternative teaching strategy because it focuses on those areas in which the child is good, strong, and competent. Our Somerville work clearly indicates that, at the very least, a child's involvement in an area of demonstrated competence means that the child will not (as is often the case) feel completely inadequate in the school environment. At best, areas of strength can be used as a means to develop academic skills and as a vehicle for self-expression.

Two years after we completed the Somerville study, we met with the four teachers once again. We observed some of their classrooms and interviewed them about the impact of the experience. We found that the Spectrum approach had indeed changed their view of children and learning in a lasting way.

"Spectrum's philosophy of looking at children's strengths is very appealing. I am now constantly thinking of my students' strengths: what he or she is good at rather than what his or her problems are," said one teacher.

Another teacher commented, "One of the most important things I learned from the Spectrum work was that you don't have to teach children everything, but that you should expose them to many things."

The third teacher said that through Spectrum she has grown to view learning as a multifaceted experience, encompassing many different fields (such as music and social understanding) and approached in many different ways (including movement and hands-on activities). The fourth teacher still was using learning centers in her classroom, opening them twice a week for one hour at a time.

In fact, in our Somerville project, Spectrum's most profound effect may have involved the teachers, helping them see *all* their students as talented individuals with the potential to learn and grow.

NOTES

1. The names of teachers, as well as those of the students, have been changed in this chapter.

2. Although there is no general consensus on the definition of "at risk," there are a number of widely mentioned symptoms, such as poverty, poor nutrition, deficiency in the English language, low self-esteem, and low academic performance (Brodinsky & Keough, 1989; Comer, 1988; Willis, 1989).

3. The second volume in this series, titled *Project Spectrum: Early Learning Activities* (Chen, 1998), is based upon these guides and incorporates teacher and student feedback.

REFERENCES

Brodinsky, B., & Keough, K. E. (1989). *Students at risk: Problems and solutions.* (Report No. ISBN-0-87652-123-5.) Arlington, VA: American Association of School Administrators. (ERIC Document Reproduction Service No. ED 306 642)

Chen, J. Q. (1993, April). *Building on children's strengths: Examination of a Project Spectrum intervention program for students at risk for school failure.* Paper presented at biennial meeting of the Society of Research in Child Development, New Orleans, LA. (ERIC Document Reproduction Service No. ED 357 847)

Chen, J. Q. (Ed.). (1998). *Project spectrum: Early learning activities.* Project Zero Frameworks for Early Childhood Education, Vol. 2. New York: Teachers College Press.

Comer, J. P. (1988). Educating poor minority children. *Scientific American, 259*(5), 42–48.

Hanushek, E. (Ed.). (1996). *Improving the performance of America's schools.* Washington, DC: National Academy Press.

Ingels, S. J., Abraham, S. Y., Karr, R., Spencer, B. D., & Frankel, M. R. (1992). *National education longitudinal study of 1988, first follow-up: Student component data file user's manual* (NCES Publication No. 92–030). Washington, DC: U.S. Department of Education.

Schorr, L. B., with Schorr, D. (1988). *Within our reach: Breaking the cycle of the disadvantaged.* New York: Anchor Books/Doubleday.

Vygotsky, L. S. (1986). *Thought and language* (A. Kozulin, Trans.). Cambridge, MA: MIT Press. (Original work published 1934)

Willis, H. D. (1989). *Students at risk: A review of conditions, circumstances, indicators, and educational implications.* Elmhurst, IL: North Central Regional Educational Laboratory.

CHAPTER 4

MAKING CONNECTIONS:
A SCHOOL–MUSEUM PARTNERSHIP

Imagine an educational setting where young students make their way through diverse learning environments, engaged in activities that nourish a range of intelligences and that cultivate the students' own unique profiles of abilities. The learning environments are realistic—a grocery store, a construction site, a health clinic—and include the tools, materials, and problems that obtain in these real-world settings. Here children learn about categorization, numbers, and weight by selecting produce, using scales, and operating cash registers; they develop mechanical problem-solving abilities and hone fine motor skills through hands-on encounters with simple machines and tools; and they play out their questions and fears about their own bodies and health by using stethoscopes, crutches, and the examination table.

In this setting, teachers work as guides, helping children articulate and answer problems in the symbol system or "language" appropriate to the context, be it math, music, or medicine. Parents are present and involved in their children's learning. Students often work cooperatively, as required by the task or problem. Is this site the ideal hypothetical Spectrum classroom? In a sense, yes, because the setting includes much of what Spectrum strives to achieve in an educational milieu: experiences across a range of intelligences, with the potential to nurture individual profiles; hands-on activities for the young child; and representations of roles linked to adult endstates, set in real-world contexts under conditions open to a range of working styles. This is a place where children can be observed doing what they like best. But it is not a Spectrum classroom, nor is it hypothetical. It's a children's museum.

SCHOOLS AND CHILDREN'S MUSEUMS:
COMPLEMENTARY MISSIONS

A new and growing phenomenon, the children's museum—like discovery centers and many science museums—includes exhibits and activities intended to engage children. Exhibit creators strive to tap into domains, skills, passions, and goals that are, by their very nature, captivating and motivating to young students. Because children have so many different tastes, interests, and abilities, the children's museum by design supports diverse combinations of intelligences (for further discussion on children's museums, see Gardner, 1991, 1993; Davis & Gardner, 1993; Falk & Dierking, 1992).

At the same time, the children's museum has explicit educational aspirations. It invites the emergence and development of a range of skills, knowledge, and literacies. Most broadly, its unique setting has the potential to draw a young clientele into the very sorts of risk taking that are at the core of the "most worthwhile adventures into learning, into the forbidding and/or enticing territory of the unknown" (Davis & Gardner, 1993, p. 37). These adventures may range from exploring new and unfamiliar regions such as a cave or a Mexican village, to taking on new roles in familiar places, such as the grocery store.

Although they actively pursue educational objectives, children's museums are not necessarily viewed by the public as institutions of learning. Instead, they are seen as places of recreation—the destination for an annual field trip or a one-time family outing. Although people might agree that children *can* learn something at the children's museum, the point of a trip there is play or entertainment. Thus the museum visit is punctuated by a rush to "see it all." A breathless, superficial sweep of the building often supplants the kind of sustained, repeated activities we associate with meaningful learning experiences. The educational potential of the children's museum may go unrealized because museums often are perceived, and therefore utilized, as indoor amusement parks.

Different Venues for Learning

Visitors to the children's museum typically don't know what they are missing, because they think of school as the place where real learning occurs. Our schools represent *the* formal system charged with educating our children. Over the course of history, a set of assumptions and practices has created the school as an establishment designed to ensure the transmission of knowledge and inculcation of skills valued in our society. Schooling is formal and to be taken seriously. Community participation and cohesion in this effort is established through organizations such as the Parent-Teacher Association and school management teams. To varying extents, schools benefit from articulated educational goals and overarching missions. Schools are held accountable for their students' learning through formal systems of assessment.

With this responsibility and accountability comes the benefit of students' regular attendance in a familiar setting, within a familiar structure, among familiar people, not the least of whom is a teacher—the same teacher for at least one school year. Teachers generally can count on this system to support their efforts to plan, teach, and assess regularly. Learning objectives can be addressed in an ongoing, long-term manner. Students are aware that learning is the explicit goal of schooling, and that learning is valued highly by adults in the school.

On the other hand, the organized, formal schooling system suffers from outmoded bureaucracy and educational practices. As the number of students has grown, attempts at efficiency have resulted in decontextualized pedagogy and assessment: a focus on the 3 Rs in and of themselves, at the expense of their use and utility in the real world. The range of skills and abilities—intelligences, if you will—that obtains in the real world is whittled down to reading, writing, and arithmetic, presented in a limited number of ways (such as lectures or drills). Although all children may be admitted to public school, few of these schools are committed or able to present material in such a way, or variety of ways, that all children will understand.

The two institutions certainly feel different to a child. Schools are generally quite restrictive (although preschools are more flexible than elementary schools); museums are almost totally free and unstructured. Too much structure can limit the child's experience; too little can dilute it, as the child launches into a new task before thinking through the previous one. In either case, the individual child can fall through the cracks.

Each institution—the school and the children's museum—has a definite educational mission. The museum offers a vast array of exhibits and resources; the school offers structure, curricula, and a daily routine in a familiar environment with familiar results. Each possesses strengths that further its educational mission and constraints that obstruct it. They make an interesting overlay; that is, where one is weak, the other is strong. It seems reasonable to assume that the two could be coupled to build on their strengths and ameliorate their limitations for the benefit and education of all children who enter them. But how?

The Spectrum Bridge

The Spectrum approach provides a natural bridge between the two institutions. Like the children's museum, the Spectrum approach tries to expand children's vision beyond school walls. Classroom activities introduce children to adult roles and careers, and demonstrate various ways that the skills being learned will be used later in life. Assessment takes place in the context of authentic tasks. Children can work with engaging materials that evoke all areas of intelligence and nourish each child's unique abilities and interests. Children have a certain degree of choice within the required classroom fare.

But like more traditional school programs, Spectrum counts on the long-term nature of the classroom to give students the sorts of ongoing, repeated experiences that successful learning requires. Learning and assessment take place in an orderly fashion throughout the school year. Students have time to explore a range of domains and to deepen their understanding; teachers have time to closely observe and build upon their students' interests, talents, and understanding.

For the Spectrum team,[1] forging an alliance between a school and a children's museum would allow us to explore how best to integrate the different resources that each institution had to offer. How could the physical resources of the museum, with its large-scale, professionally designed exhibits, be combined with the pedagogical resources of the school, with its ongoing relationship between students and professional teachers? How could the multiple "entry points" at the museum be focused to enhance the classroom curriculum? We hoped to bring the two institutions together to answer these and other questions, with the Spectrum approach offering a theoretical underpinning and a framework for planning children's passage from one learning environment to the other.

In terms of our own research, we were eager to understand Spectrum's educational implications, particularly for the creation of learning situations outside schoolhouse doors. Thus we began Spectrum's Children's Museum Project.

THE CHILDREN'S MUSEUM PROJECT

Because this was our first foray outside the school, we thought it was important to find established museum and school partners. We sought out an exemplary preschool setting and a community institution with strong commitments to children and education. We found what we were looking for in the Children's Museum in Boston and in the SMILE Program in Somerville.

SMILE (Sequentially Monitored Individualized Learning Environments) is an innovative Chapter I–funded preschool program, housed in a public elementary school. Located in a quiet, residential neighborhood, SMILE had been offering quality developmental education to young children for more than 25 years. The head teacher, Cheryl Seabrook-Wilson, thought that the Spectrum project might help her address some of her own concerns about the lack of educational opportunities for many young children.

In our search for a quality children's museum, we needed to look no further than our own backyard. The Children's Museum, located along the old channel of Boston Harbor, is one of the oldest and most outstanding children's museums in the world. It possesses the institutional experience and wherewithal to offer a variety of compelling experiences for children of all ages, learning styles, and interests. The exhibits are large-scale, interactive, and diverse. When we approached the administration we learned that the museum had been actively seeking and initiating community ties through teacher museum training, multicultural education programs, and other outreach efforts. Jeri Robinson, then director of early childhood programs at the museum and our primary collaborator, was strongly committed to the community and to the Boston-area schools. She saw the collaboration as an opportunity to further her professional and personal goals of serving the community's children.

During the initial meetings with our new museum and preschool partners, we identified the mutual goals that would shape the project. For Seabrook-Wilson, an important aim was providing children with the rich array of activities and materials needed to nurture their intelligences. Although this is a basic tenet of the Spectrum approach, many schools, like SMILE, have limited funds to spend on faculty, professional development, and supplies. Seabrook-Wilson recognized that this project would enable her to take advantage of resources at the Children's Museum that she had long recognized but had not had the opportunity to utilize.

The collaboration, explained Seabrook-Wilson, would also help "fill the gaps" of her own curriculum. Like many excellent preschool teachers, she used a theme-based curriculum that regularly included activities spanning several domains. She believed that the Spectrum approach and MI theory would help her identify and shore up those areas underrepresented in her units, particularly music and movement. She also hoped that the collaboration would provide support for her classroom aides and increase parent participation.

For our museum partners, the collaboration would provide a framework for upgrading the educational component of visits by preschool classes. The Children's Museum had long sought avenues to help visitors, especially parents, see the educational aspect of museum play, and to become involved in their children's learning process at exhibits. Visiting the Children's Museum is somewhat like going to a large educational mall in which children and their adult companions freely "shop," moving from exhibit to exhibit looking for items of interest. Because a museum visit usually is viewed as a one-time encounter, the pace is quick. Children typically spend less than a minute at each exhibit, even though many stations involve blowing bubbles, rolling balls down chutes, and other types of active participation. Robinson and her staff wanted to find a way to encourage multiple visits to the museum and more in-depth involvement in the exhibits.

For our own part, we were interested in designing instructional vehicles that could be used not just by these two institutions, but by sites across the country. We believed that the most educationally powerful vehicle for uniting the school and the museum was the creation of "resonant learning experiences," and we wanted to test this concept.

Resonant Learning Experiences

"Resonance" refers to the echoing effect that ideally will occur when children encounter the same or similar materials and activities in different settings, over time. In this format, each encounter is intended to evoke and extend the previous ones. We hoped that by creating resonant learning opportunities, in which fundamental themes and concepts were presented on a regular basis in the familiar context of school and in the novel context of the children's museum, we could help young children internalize and understand the concepts more fully. Furthermore, encountering the subject matter in a site outside school could help children realize that the topic was important to the community at large, not just to their teachers.

We hoped to include the child's home as another place where resonant learning could occur. One way to involve family members in children's education, we believed, was to help them understand how visits to a museum (either as a family or school undertaking) could be used to enrich children's learning. We also developed take-home versions of some Spectrum activities for children to perform with their families. By participating in these activities, parents and other family members could show that both the topic at hand, and schooling in general, was worthy of their time and attention. Thus the home became the the third corner of the resonance triangle.

We decided that the theme-based unit would be a useful vehicle for conveying the Spectrum and MI approach through resonant learning experiences, because it enables educators to explore a single concept with multiple activities that, over time, address the full range of intelligences and styles that each child brings to bear. Although we wanted these units to explore domains or use intelligences that often are overlooked, such as bodily-kinesthetic or intrapersonal abilities, we also wanted to include different types of activities within familiar and accepted areas—for example, by adding expressive storytelling to more typical language arts activities such as reading and dictating.

In collaboration with the museum and school staffs, we developed two thematic units: Day and Night, and All About Me. We chose these themes because we felt that they provided an ideal blend of familiarity and fascination for the preschool child. These themes were generative, that is, they not only presented concepts important to young children in specific disciplines (science and social understanding), but also prompted questions and investigations in a variety of other domains. Moreover, we would not have to start from scratch; Seabrook-Wilson previously had taught similar units that we could use as a jumping-off point, and the Children's Museum had exhibits that incorporated related concepts.

By encouraging teachers and children to focus on a single theme during visits to the children's museum, we hoped to provide a less hectic, more meaningful experience for museum patrons. We believed that once parents, teachers, and children discovered the kind of in-depth learning that could take place at museums, they would opt for thoughtful encounters at individual exhibits rather than the see-it-all race.

Kits for the School

Because we anticipated the need to move activities from one exhibit or school space to another, and from school or museum to home, we settled on the self-contained and transportable format of a kit. We packed unit materials and documentation in a clear, covered plastic tub for easy transportation, storage, and dissemination. Inside each kit was written material that included introductory information, classroom activities, take-home activities for parents to do with their children, projects based on popular children's books, and a list of related museum exhibits.

The Day and Night kit activities were developed for use at school, home, and museum, and were designed to engage all the intelligences. They included a language arts element in the form of storyboards based on stories popular with the preschool set, such as *Where the Wild Things Are* (Sendak, 1963) and *Ira Sleeps Over* (Waber, 1972). They also included science activities such as experiments with prisms and flashlights, shadow explorations, and observational studies (e.g., "What do we see in the sky during the day and at night?"). Some activities, such as the storyboards, were available for children to use on their own in the classroom over a period of several days or weeks, whereas other activities, such as those involving movement, were conducted intermittently by an adult. The thematic organization of the activities and their clear, written descriptions made it possible for classroom aides to lead movement, music, and art activities independently, without extensive teacher directions or guidance.

The museum collaboration involved about 45 children, who attended either the morning or afternoon session in the SMILE classroom. With few exceptions, the children loved the unit activities. The storyboard proved to be an especially popular activity. Four-year-old Lisa, for example, enjoyed having an adult close by, turning the pages of the book at the "right" time while she retold the story using the inviting characters and props included in the kit. Kathy preferred combining materials from two or more stories, inventing a richly detailed story of her own making.

The children also enjoyed playing a board game, created by the Spectrum staff, called Day-to-Night. The game depicted a child's day, starting with rising in the morning and ending with bedtime. Children advanced their game pieces around the board by throwing dice marked with numbers. The game consistently initiated enthusiastic conversations about familiar daily routines and activities, while giving children an engaging entry point into the often difficult domain of numbers.

Activities for the Museum

While the SMILE teaches were testing the kits in the classroom, museum staff were trying the activities three times a week in Playspace, the preschoolers' enclave inside the museum. Playspace is an enclosed indoor playground that emphasizes gross motor activities and includes a large climbing structure and play vehicles. We quickly found that the large size of the equipment and the boisterous nature of its use would overshadow the Spectrum activities, which generally required the children to sit down and use their fine motor skills. The fact that the SMILE children were already familiar with the kit activities also contributed to their lack of interest in them while they were at the museum. Moreover, the kit format, designed to make it easy for teachers, aides, and parents to administer and store the activities, did not serve similar purposes at the museum, where the activities did not need to be stored or moved extensively.

Another element of our plan proved much more successful. We identified exhibits throughout the museum that related to the day-and-night theme, particularly in regard to different aspects of light and dark. These exhibits included *Liquid Light*, in which a series of mylar strips are hung under an overhead light in such a way that they look like they are dripping or pouring; *Recollections*, in which children's shadows are projected and then "frozen" in different colors on a giant screen; and *Shadow Play*, in which children trigger a series of sounds as their shadows cross the path of a light sensor. Teachers and parent helpers were asked to bring children to these and other related exhibits during the museum visit.

To enhance resonance and also make good use of our Playspace experience, we designed age-appropriate activities that children could perform while at the exhibits. For example, at the *Dreams* exhibit museum staff led children in discussions about dreaming and ways in which the exhibit related to the children's own dream experiences. Such exhibit "add-ons" clarified the exhibit's connection to the curricular theme, and also made the exhibit more interesting and meaningful to young children. Many of the museum's exhibits had been designed for older and larger children; as a result, they were conceptually out of reach of the preschooler and relied on text to convey necessary information. The Spectrum activities gave 4- and 5-year-olds access to these exhibits.

The two strategies of identifying thematically related exhibits and adding activities there fulfilled our goal. Young children stayed longer and seemed more engaged at these exhibits than they had before. Therefore we chose to focus on these strategies for our second theme, All About Me. Among the museum exhibits related to this concept were *Bones* and *Mind Your Own Business*, both about the human body; *What if I Couldn't*, in which children explore physical disabilities by trying to maneuver a wheelchair or perform household tasks without using their fingers; and the Guterman House, a three-story exhibit recreating a Jewish American household during World War II and providing a link to the family-related activities in the unit.

We enhanced several of these exhibits with add-on activities. At *Bones*, we helped preschoolers relate the model human skeleton to their own bodies by doing body tracings, which we hung next to the skeleton. We also added growth charts to *Mind Your Own Business* to relate general information about the human body to children's own physical development, and a preschool obstacle course at *What if I Couldn't*, to help children think of actions they perform with ease from a different perspective.

In order to maximize resonant learning at the museum, we felt that it was important to work with the adults who have the most contact with visiting children—those responsible for the day-to-day educational activities of the museum. Therefore we conducted training sessions with the museum "interpreters," staff members who are stationed at the exhibits and conduct activities there. We explained the thematic units to the interpreters, walked them through the related exhibits, and discussed and reviewed the add-on activities. We also discussed the Spectrum approach and multiple intelligences theory. Through the training sessions and subsequent discussions, interpreters were prepared to conduct Spectrum activities at the exhibits and explain how the exhibits related to curricular themes that the children had explored in the classroom.

By designing activities specifically for use at the museum, we were able to capitalize on the museum's strengths, which included interactive technology and novel, large-scale activities. Dancing bones, "singing" shadow sensors, and a real, three-story house embedded within the museum made a lasting impression on the children and engaged them in a way that simply implementing the kit activities at both sites could never do. We saw preschoolers spending time at the exhibits, engaged in lively conversations and activities with exhibit interpreters and their adult companions. Our audience extended well beyond the SMILE classrooms. Three mornings a week, museum visitors as young as 3 years old, including whole classes of preschoolers from other programs, enjoyed All About Me movement and art activities led by museum staff in Playspace. At the same time, older preschoolers explored All About Me exhibits and activities in the greater museum under the guidance of Spectrum researchers.

In the SMILE classroom, children continued to participate in the activities we had created for the All About Me kits to foster the different intelligences. Children made self-portrait collages to help them reflect on their similarities and differences, participated in an obstacle course to challenge themselves physically, used smell jars and "feely" bags (bags containing "mystery" items that children try to identify by touch) to explore their senses, and created All About Me booklets that included activities that they could do at home. The teachers also glued photographs of the children onto small blocks for use as game pieces and dollhouse figures.

Inspired by the children's enjoyment of the museum, we created several museumlike activities for the classroom. For example, we added a simplified version of the museum shadow game to the Day and Night unit. Using a flashlight as backlighting, children experimented with shadowy images of themselves, which were projected onto a hanging sheet. New tools were added to the bubble area based on the museum's bubble exhibit. Through these activities we captured some of the excitement of the exhibit halls, found novel ways in which to deepen children's understanding of the curriculum, and used the Spectrum approach to fill the gaps that Seabrook-Wilson had identified in her classroom.

We wanted to make sure that the children saw the relationship between the exciting displays at the museum itself, and the work they were doing in class throughout the year. Therefore, when they visited the museum, teachers and chaperones (both parents and classroom aides) made explicit connections to the classroom themes by guiding children to the exhibits we had identified. We gave the chaperones maps, lists of related exhibits, and written information about the ways that the exhibits and classroom activities related to the curricular theme. Spectrum and museum staff members also spoke briefly about the activities and themes when the group arrived at the museum. This focus helped the chaperones resist the temptation to see it all, and better understand the link between museum "play" and school "work."

Parent Involvement

To create the third corner of the resonance triangle, we designed theme-related activities that children could take home to do with parents and siblings. These activities usually were similar to activities performed in class, so that to a certain extent, children could take on the role of teacher as they showed the activities to their parents. One take-home activity for the Day and Night unit included a mini-storyboard. Packaged in a box that doubled as the "stage," the storyboard included a book the children had read in class as well as the figures and props they would need to retell the story. Another activity included directions and materials for conducting observations of the moon with family members every night for a month, and making drawings to be shared with classmates. Children also brought home audiocassettes of songs that explored themes related to the unit, such as fear of the dark.

Drawing on their own memories of homework, SMILE parents understood the reinforcing nature of performing school-related activities at home. However, as discussed earlier in this chapter, they typically viewed the museum as a source of extracurricular activity, unrelated to formal education per se. At first, they expressed limited interest in attending a museum education session that we were offering, although when surveyed about parent education offerings, they had listed "learning how to be more actively involved in their children's education" as a major priority. SMILE parents, like most, did not identify the Children's Museum as a resource for fulfilling that priority.

We arranged for Jeri Robinson and her colleague Jane Moore, program developer in Playspace, to lead a workshop at the school. At the session, Robinson and Moore suggested strategies for guiding children through the museum during family outings. They suggested organizing each visit around a theme, especially the units that children were learning at school. They emphasized multiple visits as the key to growing comfortable with the space and achieving in-depth learning experiences at the museum.

Robinson and Moore also pointed out that parents could use the museum visit to observe their children as learners, drawing on multiple intelligences theory as a guide to evaluating their children's styles, interests, and abilities. They suggested that parents ask themselves questions such as "What observations does my child make about different bubbles? Does he or she experiment with shapes and sizes? with the wind?" These kinds of observations might help parents think of other activities that their children would enjoy pursuing at home.

The session helped parents appreciate the educational value of the museum and of the effort to link school, home, and museum activities with common curricular themes. It also gave a sense of purpose beyond mere supervision to the parents who served as chaperones on museum trips. Some parents said that they liked the maps that designated theme-related exhibits, because it helped them negotiate the museum and budget time for various exhibits. Other parents commented that they saw the connection between museum exhibits and what their children were learning in the classroom. These comments, albeit anecdotal, reflected parents' developing understanding of the children's museum as an *educational* playground with a connection to classroom activities. The parents went to the museum not only as child supervisors but as educational guides, armed with specific ideas for becoming involved with their children's learning.

Reflections on the Year

Because of the short duration of Spectrum's Children's Museum Project, we know very little about its long-term effects. We did create resonant learning experiences at school, home, and museum. And we can say that, in the short-term, children did make connections between the museum exhibits and classroom activities. For example, Bill noted similarities between the colors he saw through small prisms at the school and the dramatic effect of the lighted, moving mylar strips at the *Liquid Light* exhibit. Miranda, busy at a classroom bubble table, excitedly contrasted the scale and color of her bubbles to those in a massive bubbles exhibit at the museum. During shadow activities at the school, children referred to a similar effect found in the *Recollections* exhibit. These spontaneous comments show that children not only remembered ideas and information presented during the unit activities and at the museum, but were able to apply them in different situations and in new ways.

For Seabrook-Wilson, the Children's Museum Project offered materials and support that she needed in order to expand her instructional units in areas in which she felt least strong. Perhaps more important, the project—with the Spectrum approach and MI theory as a foundation—helped her utilize the Children's Museum in ways that were relevant and meaningful to her curriculum and students. It also provided a framework that she could continue to use to extend curricular units with visits to museums and other community resources.

For our museum partners, the Spectrum approach and the project served to develop ways in which to help parents see the educational aspect of museum play, and to become involved in their children's learning process at exhibits. With the assistance of Spectrum researchers, the museum staff was able to make some exhibits more preschool appropriate, and more evocative of the wide range of strengths and interests that children bring to the museum. The Spectrum approach seemed to elicit longer and more in-depth involvement at the exhibits and to encourage parents to come back as an educational benefit to their children.

In addition, the project has left an important legacy. Now the museum-wide director of education, Jeri Robinson continues to use the Spectrum approach to ensure a range and balance of exhibits and related activities. She also keeps MI theory in mind when designing special programs, such as theater productions. In a recent production, seven characters reminiscent of Snow White's seven dwarfs represented the different intelligences. Robinson considered this an entertaining way to express the value of different ways of learning and knowing to children and to adults, and to connect that expression with their activities at the museum.

MAKING THE MOST OF MUSEUM FIELD TRIPS

Not every school can have a one-on-one collaboration with a children's museum, but many are situated close enough to be able to visit one on a field trip. We believe that the insights we gained during our research project can help educators forge meaningful connections among school, museum, and home, and also maximize children's learning during the field trip. We would like to share a few recommendations based on what we learned.

- *Scout out the museum in advance.*

If at all possible, visit the museum yourself before you go with your class. In fact, two advance visits are best. Use the first visit to observe how other visitors, especially children, are interacting with the exhibits. Walk slowly through the museum. Which exhibits are the most popular? Which exhibits are holding the children's attention? Which exhibits attract children the same age as your students? In what ways are the children interacting with the exhibit? Keep these behaviors in mind when you go back to your classroom and observe your own students, taking note of the types of activities that engage them the most.

If possible, visit the museum again after a week. This time, experiment with and participate in the exhibits. Before you leave, find a place to sit and reflect on your experiences. Take notes on exhibits that you think might appeal to the students in your class and might enhance the curricular units you are teaching. Make sure to note the name and location of the exhibits and include a brief description.

These visits will help you get to know the physical layout of the museum, so that you can plan a sensible route through the building. In addition, once you select the exhibits that you want the children to visit, you can create resonant learning experiences by preparing pre- and postvisit activities for the classroom and home. Make sure to start the unit or previsit activities in advance of the museum trip, and to conduct follow-up activities later that will reinforce the relationship between in-school and out-of-school learning.

• *Take the children on multiple visits to the museum.*

Multiple visits enable you to focus on a limited number of exhibits, and relate these exhibits to a different classroom theme or unit on each visit. Children and parents will not feel rushed, or worry that they are missing something important or exciting, if the museum is a regular part of the curriculum. You may be able to talk with museum officials about a reduced rate.

• *Prepare your chaperones.*

Tell the chaperones why you have selected the "target" exhibits for the trip, and how these exhibits relate to what children are doing and learning in the classroom. It can be helpful to give chaperones maps showing the location of the target exhibits; if the museum provides maps, you might highlight the relevant exhibits in advance. After the visit, allow time for children and parent chaperones to reflect on their experiences together.

• *Encourage parent involvement.*

Encourage parents to go back to the museum with their children and to prompt their children to make school-exhibit connections. You can keep parents updated on classroom themes, naming related museum exhibits and suggesting follow-up activities that can be conducted at home. You do not need to prepare "take-home activity" kits; a sheet of paper with clear, user-friendly suggestions normally will suffice.

• *Use the museum visit as a catalyst.*

The museum offers a rich environment not just for parents, but also for you, the teacher, in which to watch children as they learn. Observations of your students can provide specific insights into their areas of strength and interest, and the types of activities most likely to engage their attention.

Keeping the proclivities of your students in mind, you can scan the museum for ideas to enrich your curricular units. Our visit to the Children's Museum's bubble room, for example, prompted us to add new materials for bubble blowing in the classroom. Children's museums can also provide inspiration for different environments or "corners" you can create in a classroom, such as a construction site, garden, Mexican village, rain forest, or ocean community. Although your classroom village or undersea vista may be more modest than the museum's, you can offer children the chance to participate in designing and building it. The Spectrum approach can help you frame your new activities so that they offer a range of entry points, making the theme and concepts accessible to all students.

NOTE

1. The Spectrum staff for this project included principal investigators Gardner and Feldman, along with research associates Mara Krechevsky, Valerie Ramos-Ford, Julie Viens, and Rochelle Mitlak.

REFERENCES

Davis, J., & Gardner, H. (1993, January/February). Open windows, open doors. *Museum News*, 34–37, 57–58.

Falk, J., & Dierking, L. (1992). *The Museum experience*. Washington, DC: Whalesback Books.

Gardner, H. (1991). *The unschooled mind: How children think and how schools should teach*. New York: Basic Books.

Gardner, H. (1993). *Multiple intelligences: The theory in practice*. New York: Basic Books.

Sendak, M. (1963) *Where the wild things are*. New York: Harper & Row.

Waber, B. (1972). *Ira sleeps over*. Boston: Houghton Mifflin.

Waterfall, M., & Grusin, S. (1989). *Where's the me in museum: Going to museums with children*. Arlington, VA: Vandamere Press.

CHAPTER 5

MAKING CONNECTIONS: THE SPECTRUM APPROACH TO MENTORSHIP

Not long ago, a teacher involved in a school reform project was interviewing her students. She asked one 7-year-old, "Why do you go to school?" The perplexed child replied, "I thought *you* knew!"

Initially we may chuckle at the image of this child stunned to think that perhaps he needn't have been going to school. After all, if the *adults* didn't know why he was going to school, who did? And why bother?

Unfortunately, the child's lack of awareness of why he goes to school—and his assumption that he only goes because parents and teachers require him to—are neither unique nor surprising. Most students cannot give good reasons for attending school; any significance that school once held has been lost for many. The school experience itself typically is mute on how it will benefit the student, and the prevalence of a narrow academic purview in many classrooms gives students little reason to be interested or involved in classroom fare. Of particular note is that children rarely have the opportunity to engage in schoolwork that is connected to the real world, or to see a connection between their own interests, skills, and passions and those valued in life outside the classroom.

It has long been established that children at risk do not benefit from school-based support alone. Such support also must be tied to home, community, and social service agencies. For example, the pathbreaking work of James Comer (1980) has documented that when school personnel work closely with individuals in the community, social service agencies, and the home, there is a positive effect on students' social and psychological well-being that eventually leads to higher academic achievement.

Comer's work points to the compelling need to "share expertise" among school staff and neighborhood resources—storekeepers, police officers, businesspeople—all as part of a concerted effort to reinforce in a vivid and practical way the experiences in the classroom. Absent this broader community support, some of the lessons of school, including the value of education, are not well reinforced (see also Damon, 1990; Heath, 1983).

Our earlier work with Spectrum had shown that emphasizing connections to the "real world"—for example, by introducing problems and materials drawn from everyday situations; by making available a wide range of domains connected to adult roles or careers; and by showing children that they can use their unique profiles of intelligence to solve problems and fashion products—can be highly motivating to students. We also learned that working in their areas of strengths helps students become more self-directed, better behaved, and more engaged (see Chapter 3).

Given the positive affective and educational effects of connecting the classroom to the wider world, we were convinced that well-crafted learning experiences linking schools with community resources would be an important element in school reform. The Children's Museum Project was one step in this direction. The next phase of our research, called Spectrum Connections, emerged as we pursued the notion of creating classrooms and learning experiences that look and feel more like the real world.

LAYING THE FOUNDATIONS FOR MENTORSHIPS

As is the nature of university research projects, the faces of Project Spectrum changed once again, for this its final year. Codirectors Howard Gardner and David Feldman remained at the helm; Mara Krechevsky, project manager, and Julie Viens, senior researcher, also remained and were joined by Nathan Finch, an elementary teacher with 8 years of experience in urban school settings, and Amy Deitz, a recent Tufts University graduate with a passion for and experience working with high-risk youth.

We had a single school year to design and implement a program that would build on the Spectrum approach and make classroom experiences more consonant with vocational and avocational worlds. We decided that a mentorship program would provide the best vehicle for achieving our goals. Why a mentorship program? Crucial to making substantive connections with the real world are relationships with and experiences provided by *people* in the community. Children need to be able to interact with adults who are both knowledgeable and enthusiastic about their particular areas of strength or interest. Children also need experiences that are appropriate to their age and that continue beyond a one-time exposure.

Mentorship programs involve adults working with students, typically one-on-one and on a weekly basis. The familiar image of the mentor is an adult who plays three important roles: giving academic support such as tutoring, serving as a role model for actions and values, and providing the attention and care lacking in many children's lives. Most often, traditional mentorship programs emphasize the development of close, personal relationships that help the child achieve educational goals and gain self-esteem and confidence (see Abell Foundation, Inc., 1989a, 1989b). We believed that couching the Spectrum approach within a mentorship program would provide a personalized context in which students could get to know the real world outside their classroom through real people who represent it.

At the same time, our specific goals for building school-community connections and for using the Spectrum approach as an organizing framework distinguished Connections from other mentorship programs. We planned to focus our initiative on the range of cognitive abilities and styles that existed among adults in children's own communities and that each child demonstrated. Therefore, we planned to use an MI framework both to identify children's abilities and interests and to identify mentors who represented a range of adult roles and careers. Mentor and student strengths and interests would serve as the linchpin, the guiding context, of their activities together.

We felt that this cognitive connection would lend special meaning to the program for the children. We planned whole-group mentor experiences for the first half of the year so that all children would experience a wide range of authentic adult roles that are valued in their community. In the second half of the year, we planned to give each child the opportunity to work closely and regularly with a mentor who shared—through his or her vocation or avocation—an area of interest or strength with that child. Perhaps most distinctively, mentors also would serve as teachers, leading activities related to their areas of expertise.

We considered the domain-based mentor-child experiences to be akin to traditional apprenticeships, providing students with active and sustained participation in long-term relationships with domain experts. Students would have the opportunity to observe experts, acquire firsthand experience in domain skills and concepts, and develop their capacities to use these skills and concepts in appropriate ways (Gardner, 1991).

As in our previous work, we focused on the early primary years as an important transitional time, when children move either to a first-time school experience or from preschool to a more structured formal school setting. We selected classrooms in the first and second grades. Although a domain-based mentorship program with children as young as 6 may seen unusual, we felt that making connections between school and the adult world through authentic hands-on activities was in actuality *especially* appropriate for young children.

The point was not to track children into or prepare them for particular careers, a notion antithetical to the Spectrum approach. Rather, we saw adult mentors as bringing a range of domains, skills, and passions to make the classroom more real world and the real world more meaningful to the students early in their school experience. We hoped that regular interaction with mentors would enrich the students' classroom experiences and help each student discover the answer to the question, "Why *do* I go to school?"

Establishing Connections

Children's lack of connection with the adult community and the world of work is often exacerbated in the inner city, where unemployment is high and work sites are increasingly rare. Moreover, many schools in the inner city are too financially strapped to provide minimal, let alone a variety of, experiences and resources for their students. (Kozol, 1991). Therefore we decided to work with a school in Boston's central city.

To select the site, we sent letters to 20 principals, met with representatives from the 10 schools that responded with interest, and conducted follow-up classroom observations and interviews with teachers at five schools. We decided to partner with the Samuel P. Mason Elementary School, one of the smallest and most economically impoverished schools in the city's public school system. Set in a warehouse and shipping district, the Mason School is tucked between two residential neighborhoods in Boston's Roxbury community. Much of the school's population is drawn from housing projects there and in nearby South Boston. Violence and drugs are prevalent in the neighborhoods in which most of the children and their families live.

The Mason School serves many children who were identified as at risk for school failure for a variety of reasons; at the time of the project, 79% of the Mason School's students were eligible for free and reduced-price breakfast and lunch programs, and at least 65% came from single-parent homes. Although economically poor, the Mason School was rich in diversity, with a population that included African American (42%), Cape Verdian (23%), White (19%), Puerto Rican (15%); and Asian (1%) students. Approximately half spoke languages other than English at home.

Another Mason School strength was its dedicated and motivated staff. In the 2 years since Mary Russo, Mason's energetic and forward-looking principal, had headed the school, the student population had doubled to 260 students. Under Russo's guidance, the school had undertaken a schoolwide reform effort with school-based management at its center. Russo had organized an active group of parents to participate. We took advantage of the Mason School's parent involvement by forming a Connections Parent Advisory Council.

Our teacher collaborators were two motivated and experienced teachers, Gwen Stith and Mary O'Brien, first- and second-grade teachers, respectively, and Lindsay Trementozzi, Stith's talented student teacher. This threesome strongly believed that their students possessed a myriad of untapped abilities, but felt that they had few resources with which to draw out and nurture these strengths. The Connections program seemed to offer a way to do this by expanding the scope of, rather than watering down, the academic curriculum.

We began holding biweekly meetings with the Mason teachers in the spring, to introduce them to the Spectrum approach. Meetings and miniworkshops continued throughout the summer. Since teachers planned to use MI theory to make and record student observations as soon as school started in the fall, much time was spent discussing the purposes and techniques of classroom observations. Agreeing that the richest observations are drawn, logically, from the richest activities, we devoted an important part of our sessions together to identifying such activities and creating some anew.

Selecting the Mentors

Teachers and researchers agreed that we wanted to identify mentors from different professions, in order to introduce children to a range of adult role models and to enable each child to work closely with a mentor in a shared area of interest or strength. We also wanted a group that reflected children's cultural or ethnic backgrounds and provided a balance of males and females.

To select our mentors, we devised and implemented a comprehensive application and review process. We drew on the expertise of local mentorship organizations, including Boston Partners in Education (BPE) and Boston United Way's One to One Program. With 25 years of experience in mentorship programming, BPE in particular provided us with invaluable expertise in identifying and screening mentors. We made dozens of calls to organizations and individuals, and to those who expressed interest, we sent an application packet that included background information and an application form. After screening the responses, we selected and interviewed candidates to assess their competence in working with young children and their ability to make a commitment to the program. We also considered whether each candidate's field or avocation was compatible with the first- and second-grade curricula (see Figure 5.1 for interview questions).

By summer's end we had identified our core group of 10 mentors, warm and talented individuals who were willing to commit a substantial amount of time to participate in the program. We were delighted to find

FIGURE 5.1. Sample Interview Questions for Mentor Applicants

1. Please tell us about your current job (or the work you will be talking about and sharing with the children).

   How long have you been working there?

   What are the skills that you need in order to do what you do?

   How would you describe your work to 6- or 7-year-olds?

   What part of your job would kids find most interesting?

   What are the most useful things children might learn from finding out about your work?

2. Please talk a little more about why you want to be a mentor. What do you hope to get out of this experience?

3. Do you have experience working with children 6 or 7 years old? If so, what were the best memories and most frustrating experiences you have had with children this age?

4. What do you think might be the benefits and difficulties of working with small groups of children, as opposed to working with an individual child?

5. What would you do if

   -you were leading a small group activity and one child refused to participate?

   -you were working with a small group of children and one child could not sit still —in fact, was so disruptive that it was hard for the other children to work?

   -you were working with a child who was writing an autobiographical story, and the child shared with you a very disturbing moment from his or her home life?

6. What concerns do you have about being a mentor? What issues do you think we haven't considered?

7. Please tell us more about the clubs, organizations, or both in which you are currently involved. What (other) kinds of things do you do in your free time that you might be able to share with children?

8. (Explain time commitment, including training.) Do you think you can keep this commitment?

such a diverse and enthusiastic group. We also were fortunate to capitalize on the Mason School's proximity to and fledgling partnership with the Boston Parks and Recreation Department (BPR). This agency was virtually across the street from the school, and several of its employees had participated in a reading program at the school in previous years. Of our 10 mentors, 6 were BPR employees who were given release time to participate in the program during the workday.

In terms of the professions represented, the BPE mentors included two urban planners (one was also an architect), two park rangers, and two athletes. Our other four mentors were a musician, a poet, a video artist, and a photographer. We brought together a diverse group of African American, White, Indian, and multiracial individuals, including eight males. We would have liked a more gender-balanced group, but were nonetheless pleased to provide such positive male role models representing a variety of professions.

Designing the Curriculum

In order for children to grasp the school-community link, mentor visits would have to become an integral part of the classroom curriculum. We decided to introduce the mentors to the students within the context of a study of the community, with an emphasis on the local neighborhood. We planned three intersecting units to be conducted from September through mid-January.

The year would begin with a familiar primary unit, All About Me, followed by All About My Family. During the third unit, All About My Community/Neighborhood, most of the mentors would make initial, whole-group visits to the classrooms and explain their professional roles within the community. In constructing the units, we drew on the teachers' repertoire of activities as well our own, such as the All About Me activities developed during the museum collaboration. As described in Chapter 2, Spectrum shares certain elements with the project approach, and we also turned to that literature to guide the development of unit activities (Jacobs, 1989; Katz & Chard, 1989; Zimiles, 1987; see also Gardner, 1991, pp. 51–52, regarding the project approach).

We incorporated the Spectrum approach into the Connections program in a variety of ways. First, as described above, we identified mentors who represented a range of abilities. Second, we used the Spectrum approach as a framework to develop and modify unit activities that appealed to a range of students' strengths and interests. Third, we drew heavily on Spectrum activities and their related observational frameworks to assess student strengths and interests. For example, the Spectrum Assembly and

Storyboard activities were integrated into classroom activities to provide a purposeful look at children's mechanical and expressive language abilities.

Fourth, as a carryover from the school-museum collaboration, we strove to create resonant learning experiences, those "echoing" experiences meant to reinforce children's learning. Thus, Connections activities included unit activities, preparatory and follow-up activities around the mentor visits, and the mentor visits themselves, most centered around the neighborhood and community theme.

Stith and O'Brien also decided to include learning centers in their classrooms, which provided an ever present context for Connections-related materials and experiences. Materials that related to upcoming and previous mentor visits were rotated through the learning centers. Spectrum assessment activities also found a home there. The learning centers gave the teachers the chance to observe children more closely in the different domains and provided the children with the opportunity to familiarize themselves with the "tools" of the mentors' trades.

Training the Mentors

Our first mentor training session was held in September and was co-facilited by Lonnie Carton of Boston Partners in Education. A child development expert with years of experience in the Boston public schools, Carton was another benefit of our collaboration with the BPE. The first training session was a time for all of us to meet one another and cover a multitude of issues, from child development and the theoretical basis of the Spectrum approach, to practical information about the Mason School, the curriculum, the background of the children, and accepted rules and practices.

Five mentor training sessions were held over the year. These meetings were used for discussing and modeling practical concerns, such as how to use group management techniques to maintain an orderly classroom environment; to consider the more difficult issues of working with at-risk and troubled children; and to address any specific issues that were identified during mentor visits, such as handling behavior problems and applying instructional strategies.

From the first session forward we stressed that Spectrum Connections was an unusual and probably more challenging proposition for the mentors than were most mentorship programs, because we were asking them not only to be a friend and role model to children, but to actually *teach* the children domain-based skills. Therefore, we allotted time during each session for the mentors to work on creating the activities they would conduct with the students. This gave mentors an opportunity to seek teaching support and ideas from the teachers, Project Spectrum and BPE staff members, and their fellow mentors.

As in any group, the mentors' ability to establish a rapport with their students varied widely. Whereas some of the mentors could easily gauge the interest level of their students, others needed assistance throughout the year in making their work accessible to first graders. The availability of teacher and staff support was crucial to the success of the program.

Asked to evaluate the training program, the mentors reported that the sessions were useful and important for a number of reasons. They found the information regarding child development, instruction, and management techniques particularly useful. They noted that the sessions helped build relationships among Connections' partners. They also appreciated the chance to see student biographical sketches and collections of student work as a way of getting to know the students. The training sessions were useful to Spectrum staff as well, helping us gauge where we could intervene most beneficially.

INTRODUCING THE MENTORS AND THEIR AREAS OF EXPERTISE

Biweekly, whole-group mentor visits began in early October. All the mentors came at least once, twice if they visited both classrooms. The neighborhood unit served as an effective lead-in to the mentors and their community roles, just as we had hoped. For example, studying city structures during a "buildings walk" led naturally to the urban planner visits. Before musician Ron Reid's visit, students explored the question "Where do we hear music in our community?"

Children's eagerness to participate and the high quality of their work suggest that the Connections instructional units were engaging to students. Children's work was especially detailed and carefully executed when the tasks at hand were relevant to their daily lives, such as those involving the parks near their homes, their favorite music, or hands-on explorations.

Before mentors came, students participated in preparatory activities led by the teacher or made available at the learning centers. For example, in advance of the musician's visit, students studied different instruments and listened to and discussed different types of music. At the learning centers, they made sound cylinders by filling film canisters with small items such as beans and paper clips, and experimented with the different sounds they made.

Children also were given time at the learning centers for free exploration with tools and other materials provided by the mentors. For example, in preparation for the urban planner visits, teachers set up the mechanical learning station with a T-square, blue-prints, and other architectural and design tools. We found that domain materials such as these generated a great deal of curiosity about and questions for the mentor before their visits and a high level of activity in the learning centers afterwards.

To ensure their active participation in the mentor visit, children were asked to brainstorm questions in advance. Their questions usually started off with general fare such as "When were you born?" and "Do you have kids?" Teachers helped students prepare more-domain-specific questions, so that they could ask the musician, "How did you learn how to play drums?" and the city planner/architect, "Can you make maps?" At the suggestion of Spectrum staff, mentors followed a flexible but consistent format for their presentations: "Who am I?" (a personal introduction), "What do I do?" (introduction to the domain), "What do you want to know?" (a question-and-answer session), and "What does it look like?" (a hands-on activity).

When Ron Reid, bass and steel-drum musician, came to the class-room, he moved quickly to playing his instruments for the obviously rest-less group. Children applauded with genuine delight and were happy to share their thoughts: "It sounded like a horse! "I've never seen a guitar like *that* before!" As was the case with all mentors, there was no shortage of questions, "What are those you're playing the drums with?" (rubber-tipped mallets); "What's your job?" (musician); "How did you learn to play?" Reid answered some questions, while turning others over to the students themselves: "You tell me, what would *you* do if you wanted to learn to play an instrument?"

For his hands-on activity, Reid taught the children a short calypso song and accompanying gestures and dance steps. Then, he helped each child try to play the steel drums. During his visit, photographer Reggie Jackson brought in cameras and other equipment and had students create images using photographic paper. The athlete mentors engaged students in movement activities (see Figure 5.2 for examples of mentor visits and related activities).

Like Reid, most mentors brought in domain-related tools and materi-als. One park ranger brought in a horse-grooming kit a week before his visit, and then brought a horse on the day of his visit! The other park ranger arrived fully outfitted with gear that fascinated the students (walkie-talkie, uniform, badges, etc.); the city planners left the drafting tools in the learning station for several weeks and brought maps for the whole-group visit.

Ideas raised during the mentor visits were pursued with follow-up ac-tivities during group instruction and learning center time. After Reid's

FIGURE 5.2. Examples of Mentor Visits and Related Activities

Mentor	Previsit Activities	Mentor Visit	Post-Visit Activities	Learning Center
AMATUL HANNAN Video Artist/ Actress	Discuss diversity using photos Discuss children's special qualities Brainstorm questions	Discuss Amatul's artwork, video work and its treatment of diversity Make "I Am Special" shirts Videotape event with special effects by Amatul	View video Construct "big book" with illustrated stories about the visit	Draw and paint Read books, listen to cassettes about being "special" Read "big book"
RON REID Musician/Band Leader	Make sound cylinders, maracas Make pitched instruments by filling glasses with different amounts of water Discuss instrument poster Listen to music, identify instruments Brainstorm questions	Discuss Ron's instruments, how to learn to play, music school, how steel drums are made Demonstrate steel drums/bass Teach children song/gestures Children play steel drum	Write and draw reflection sheets; make them into book Hold group discussion: What is music? What is a musician? Discuss Ron's visit	Use sound cylinders and maracas for rhythm games, sound matching Play with water-glass instruments Listen to music tapes, review instruments on poster
VINEET GUPTA Architect/ Urban Planner	Discuss pictures of playgrounds and equipment Build structures with marshmallows and toothpicks Observe Boston skyline Take walking tour, notice buildings Use Vineet's tools	Discuss Vineet's job planning parks Examine his maps Try out his tools In small groups, make models of "the best park in the world" using recyclables, junk items	Write and draw reflection sheets; make them into book Visit Grade 1 constructions Continue working on constructions	Play with building blocks, Construx, and other building materials Play with grinders, assembly materials Start building city

95

visit, students went on "sound walks" exploring the different "musical" sounds in their neighborhood; after the city planners' visits, students continued to work on construction projects. Children also were encouraged to write and draw their reflections after each mentor visit. This exercise helped children develop writing and thinking skills, as well as make their own school-community connections. The second-grade children produced several books containing laminated reflection sheets based on each visit.

Matching Students and Mentors by Areas of Interest

The mentors' commitment would intensify during the second half of the year, when they would work once a week with the same small group of students. So that we could match each student with the most appropriate mentor, we spent much time during the early months of the school year trying to identify students' strengths and interests.

As in the previous phases of Spectrum, we assumed that children would demonstrate a distinctive profile of abilities and interests if presented with a broad enough set of experiences. Our primary tool for identifying student strengths was a program of observations conducted during the unit activities, the biweekly mentor encounters, and the learning station activities, which included several Spectrum assessments. The students' reflections on mentor visits and activities, as well as parent and student interviews, supplemented the observations as a resource for identifying students' proclivities.

We reviewed the observations and other sources during Spectrum-teacher meetings, structuring our conversations around such questions as

- What abilities and interests did particular students demonstrate and how?
- In what activities did particular students excel?
- To what curricular and Spectrum activities were particular students drawn?
- To which mentors were particular students drawn?
- During which activities did particular students help others?

Stith and O'Brien appreciated these discussions and the emphasis on what the children *could do*. The teachers acknowledged that they typically spent far too much time having to identify student weaknesses. They appreciated the opportunity to look for things that kids were good at and to have the context and resources with which to respond to student strengths and interests.

The teachers described these meetings as professional-development activities, activities through which they learned how to observe closely, observe for multiple intelligences, and focus on strengths. They noted that they were learning how to organize their classrooms around students' strengths and interests. And as the teachers observed the range of their students' emerging abilities, they also recognized that some domains were not represented in their classrooms, and set out to make room for activities and materials in those disciplines.

By early January each child was placed with a mentor whom we had assessed as a "best match" to that child's interests and abilities. Groups ranged in size from three to six children per mentor. The size and composition of each group depended on students' identified strengths and interests, as well as on particular considerations such as avoiding obvious personality conflicts between children. By mid-January, the small-group mentor experiences began (for a chronology of the Connections program, see Figure 5.3). Our assessment appeared effective: only one child was clearly unhappy with his group, because he was the only boy. He was moved to another group the following week.

Working Together

> It's a spring mentor day in the first grade. Amatul Hannan, video artist, is in one corner of the classroom helping her four lively charges trace templates for the storyboard for their video project. Across the room Aldo Ghirin, urban planner, and his group of three are engrossed in designing and building a classroom model. Downstairs in the teachers' lounge, park ranger John Piasta's group of three huddles over the contents of "collection cans," trying to distinguish which of their found objects are "natural" and which are "fabricated"; really do belong on the ground and which are "pollution." Around the corner athlete-mentor Leo Boucher leads a group of children as they create an obstacle course using mats, hula hoops, and large foam squares.

Mentor days were always exciting; energy began to build in the classroom long before the mentors showed up. Without a firm grasp of time, some first graders asked all week, "Is this mentor day?" and then all day, "When are the mentors coming?" Mentors visited the first-grade class for an hour on Wednesday; the second-grade class, for an hour on Thursday.

Spectrum staff and teachers helped mentors shape their activities into month-long units, with each activity building on skills that children had learned the previous week. For example, Hannan worked on a long-term video project with her first-grade group. After deciding to make a music video, the children created storyboards to map out the sequence of songs,

FIGURE 5.3. Chronology of Spectrum Connections

Phase 1 - Summer	Phase 2 - Fall/Winter	Phase 3 - Winter/Spring	Phase 4 - Spring/Summer
Conduct ongoing teacher training	Conduct mentor-training session	Conduct second mentor training session	Conclude small-group visits (mid-May)
Develop introductory units	Begin introductory units	Complete whole-group visits (January)	Hold culminating events: mini-Olympics, presentations, etc.
Plan mentor training	Begin whole-group mentor visits	Match children and mentors (end of January)	Hold appreciation events: Mason School breakfast; reception at Project Zero
Contact mentor organizations	Implement pre- and postvisit activities and learning centers	Develop recommended domain units	Conduct Parent Advisory Council meetings
Write and call potential mentors	Observe children	Begin small-group mentor visits	Conduct final interviews with teachers, principal, students, parents, mentors
Interview and screen applicants	Hold mentor-support session	Initiate weekly mentor support phone calls; hold mentor-support sessions	Begin data analysis
Identify mentors	Continue meetings of teachers and Spectrum researchers	Continue observations	
	Hold introductory session for parents	Continue meetings of teachers and Spectrum researchers	
		Invite parents to mentor groups	
		Hold follow-up session for parents	

dances, and special effects. They selected music, choreographed dance routines, designed and sewed colorful costumes, and learned how to use video equipment. After weeks of practice, they videotaped their performance and visited the studio where the tape was edited for their final presentation.

Children in Reggie Jackson's group mastered a variety of skills in order to produce a set of photographs. During the first few weeks, the children made cameras from oatmeal containers and coffee cans and used them to study the basic elements of photography. Then the children developed their own photographs in a makeshift darkroom at the school. As another long-range project, park rangers worked with students on a series of plant experiments in which they tried to grow beans under a variety of conditions. In one experiment, children investigated whether a bean seed could sprout if the soil was covered with a thin film of plaster of Paris. Jimmy, a boy who usually acted bored during class, was so curious about the results that he checked the growing closet every time his teacher turned her back. "I've never seen a child so focused like that," she said.

The Connections program included other activities designed to introduce the children to community resources. Museum of Fine Art (MFA) educators visited both classrooms to talk about museums and lead the students in arts projects. The children then visited the MFA and the Museum of Contemporary Art.

Both the first- and second-grade classrooms also took a field trip to the zoo at Boston's Franklin Park, with each group doing activities related to their domain. Reid's group listened for and recorded the sounds of nature; poet Lena Saunders's group found a comfortable spot under a tree in which to write poetry, using their surroundings as inspiration; Hannan's group took video footage for their project, while Jackson's group shot photographs.

Each group also took its own field trip to the mentor's work site. Individual groups visited a video studio, a college photography studio, an urban planner's office, the Parks and Recreation offices, a ranger station and stables, and a music college. These work-site field trips were one of the most successful aspects of the program. The effectiveness of the trips was due in part to the comfort that mentors felt at their own work sites, where they were the experts. Reid's group visited college practice rooms, played instruments, and observed a brass ensemble rehearsal. Andrew, one of the more troubled and unresponsive children in the classrooms, had often abandoned his group mentally or even physically; but on this field trip he stood in rapt attention when the brass ensemble played its fanfare. During his final interview, the one substantive comment that Andrew volunteered was his recollection that people played the horns and other instruments during the trip.

There were many other examples of the lasting impressions that the site visits made on the children. Angie, a member of the urban planner's group, chose to create a model of the mentor's office for her final project. The reflection sheets of the children in the photography group repeatedly included the enlarger they had seen demonstrated during their visit to the photography studio. We conducted final interviews with 26 children who made site visits. When asked what they remembered about their mentor group, 10 children immediately reported their site visits and 20 could readily name their mentor's workplace. Moreover, all but 4 easily identified their mentor's occupation. Six of the eight mentors we interviewed recommended that more visits to their work or related sites be included in the program. They felt that the visits provided the most concrete and comfortable segue into the world of work.

After each small-group mentor experience, the children completed reflection sheets that asked two questions: "What did you do?" and "What did you learn?" We encouraged children to write and draw their reflections. For the children, completing the reflection sheets was both challenging and rewarding. The exercise demanded that children reflect on and articulate their mentor activities, something that did not come easily for all children. They often used these reflections during sharing times as prompts and visual aids. At the end of the year, children pored over the entries in their completed set of reflections, bound and decorated books that they proudly carried home.

Students also kept individual portfolios, large folders made from 18" by 24" sheets of construction paper, stapled together and decorated by the children. The portfolios safely saved ongoing mentorship project work, such as mini-Olympic plans, poem drafts, model designs, and reflection sheets, from one week to the next. All groups maintained "group boxes," boxes that served as repositories for raw materials or for items too large to fit in the portfolios. For example, Reid's group kept the instruments they'd fashioned in their box.

Portfolios were one way of showing children that their work was valuable; another was the weekly sharing time, when children updated their classmates on their group's activities. They also displayed the materials they used and the products they created, from poems, to cameras, to classroom models. They often took items from their portfolios and group boxes when making their presentations. This was a notable time for teachers to assess children's content knowledge and ability to articulate their experiences and understandings. Even reticent children were motivated to speak to their peers, probably because the discussion pertained to experiences in which they were comfortable and "expert." Students typically were interested and attentive during the sharing times, and O'Brien and Stith felt that the children were learning a great deal from one another.

In addition to these more formal reflection times, the classrooms often erupted in spontaneous sharing activities immediately following mentor visits. Children asked other mentors and their peers questions about their mentor group activities. This informal questioning period gave children the opportunity to interact with adults and peers outside their own groups.

O'Brien, Stith, and Trementozzi constantly sought ways in which to integrate mentor activities into other classroom activities. They made activities and materials that were related to mentor domains available in learning centers on a regular basis. In addition, they tapped mentor group expertise whenever possible; O'Brien, for example, asked students working with the poetry mentor to share their expertise in rhyming during language arts lessons. The children themselves also made connections between their mentor group activities and their classroom lessons. During math and science lessons, one urban planner group volunteered knowledge about measurement and shapes gained from their model-building experiences. They were proud to be able to help teach their peers how to use a ruler.

BENEFITS AND CHALLENGES OF THE
MENTORSHIP PROGRAM

As we watched students and mentors work together over the course of the year, the most palpable theme we saw emerge in the Connections Project was Spectrum's effectiveness as an alternative approach to educating young children who are bored or struggling with school. Students who teachers characterized as uninvolved or "low level" were highly engaged during mentor visits and related activities. Students who typically disrupted or refused to participate in regular classroom activities would actively take part in and cooperate with their mentor groups. They comfortably conversed with their mentors, asked questions, shared ideas and strategies, and at times took on leadership roles. Trementozzi described a student in Hannan's group:

> I've seen someone like Shondra, who never talked in class, be absolutely boisterous in Amatul's group. . . . By the end of the year she was actually raising her hand and volunteering information. . . . [Before,] she would

never speak in front of the group. I really think a lot of that began with Amatul.

Children who teachers identified as being "hard to reach" spent a great deal of time in the learning centers related to their mentor group. Stith noted that Andrew, the child in Reid's group who was hard pressed to talk or partipate during most school activities, frequented the music station where he spent "an inordinate amount of time" playing instruments, playing back audiotapes from his group, and demonstrating to other children the group's homemade instruments.

Whether or not they are designated "at risk" or "difficult," all children are different; they are cognitively diverse and display a variety of strengths that can be recognized and nurtured in the classroom (Gray & Viens, 1994). By bringing mentors into the school, we attempted to show children that individuals with many different abilities are valued by, and contribute to, their communities—and that the children had the potential to make contributions of their own.

Effective Program Components

During the year, Spectrum researchers made observations of the mentors leading activities, and, as explained earlier, teachers made observations of students. We also conducted pre- and postprogram interviews with children, mentors, parents, teachers, and the principal. On the basis of this documentation, we tried to identify some of the most effective components of the program. These included developing personal relationships, fostering social skills, helping children recognize their own strengths, acquiring skills in a domain, and connecting school to the world.

Developing personal relationships. Although focusing on mentor domains and related activities, we still had wanted to maintain the close, personal relationships between mentors and children that is a hallmark of traditional mentorship programs. We felt that small groups and a flexible format for activities allowed such relationships to grow. We tried to balance the domain-based work with time for play, ensuring that mentors and children had opportunites to share activities for the sake of enjoyment and relationship building.

Mentors' and children's comments attested to our belief that we were successful in maintaining the affective, along with the cognitive, mentor-child relationships. In describing their relationships with the children, the mentors used words such as "friend," "sister," "special aunt," as often as "guide," "instructor" and "teacher." The children also expressed deep at-

tachment to the mentors in actions as well as words. When asked what he would do if he had more time to spend with his mentor, Mike responded, "I would give John a million hugs!"

Fostering social skills. Connections seemed to be responsible for other, more broadly felt effects. Mentors and teachers noted that the children's communication and interpersonal skills developed through the program. Mentors commented that the students in their group generally became very comfortable talking with them "like friends." Principal Russo re- marked that the Connections children stood out in the after-school pro- gram "in their ability to speak to adults in a comfortable, pleasant way." Several parents noted that their children talked more about school, partic- ularly about their mentor group activities.

Children truly seemed to open up with their mentors, to "come out of their shells," as one teacher described it. Two parents credited the pro- gram with helping their extremely shy daughters become less reticent and more interactive at school. O'Brien commented, "Lydia came in as a shy little bud but soon she was able to sit down and talk to Reggie and carry on a conversation and she wasn't able to do that before."

Helping children recognize their own strengths. Children gained insight into their own strengths and interests through the Connections Project. Par- ents reported that children initiated mentor-related activities at home, such as practicing physical challenges introduced in the athlete groups. Tonya, a member of Reid's group, commented that she was "good at sing- ing and hearing the beat." Louisa noted that she learned that there was "something I never knew I was good at! Making poems. I didn't know I could." Lawrence ripped his jacket in school and after an initial panic announced elatedly, "But I know how to sew! I can fix it!"

Acquiring skills in a domain. Because teaching was such a new experience for many of the mentors, the extent to which they led activities that could be classified as domain related varied. Nevertheless, it was clear that chil- dren learned a great deal about the work in which they were involved, and that they did acquire domain-based knowledge and skills in their weekly project work with the mentors. The young photographers could use tech- nical equipment, explain readily how cameras work, discuss why certain of their pictures did or did not come out, and describe and carry out the steps of developing photographs. Hannan's group also became technology savvy, whereas Saunders's poetry group became more proficient at crafting words, to which their collection of poems attested.

The two park ranger groups learned about nature and the environment; about pollution and how to grow plants. One child's mother reported that, at her son's request, she gave him a section of the garden in which to plant his own items. Hannan was excited to see one of her students combine the range of skills needed to draw a story in sequence:

> She drew a disk, a sun disk, getting closer and closer, larger and larger, and also moving from left to right— and [she drew it] very perfectly, like an animation almost. Tonya loved "This Little Light of Mine" so she drew out a script for it, in visuals. And she knew how to do a linear sequence that made sense, which is sophisticated, very sophisticated.

We also saw "basic skills" emerge in the motivating context of completing work in a domain: the use of rulers and knowledge of shapes in the course of making scale models of buildings, oral and written language skills through sharing sessions and reflection sheets, and the development of social skills, such as cooperation and sharing, through working together in groups. Less "typical" skills emerged as well in the process of the domain projects, including sewing and drawing fundamentals.

Connecting school to the world. The teachers felt that the program was helping their students demonstrate an understanding of and connection to the wider world. "It just widens their horizons," said Stith. "It widens their knowledge of who they are. It widens their knowledge of the community . . . it widens their knowledge of the city and workplaces, and how other adults are functioning." Even after working with a single mentor for the better part of the school year, half of the 38 children interviewed could identify other groups' activities, and 22 could name other mentors' professions.

Children also seemed to be finding an answer to the first question posed in this chapter, concerning the reasons they go to school. When asked what he had learned from his mentor, Max responded, "People have to go to certain schools to do certain jobs. Just like other people learn how to do a good job. They learn it in school. They go to college. I learned about it from Reggie—he brung us to his college."

Responses From Parents and Teachers

Perhaps it was children's recently honed domain-based abilities and skills, their enthusiasm for the program and their mentors, and their newfound self-awareness that accounted for parents' overwhelmingly positive response to Connections, and for an atmosphere that Russo described as "a greatly enhanced relationship between parents and the school." Russo noted that the Connections Parent Advisory Council, the parent informational meetings we offered, and the invitations we extended to parents to visit mentor groups all built a bridge between parents and the school. To be sure, it was parents who picked up the torch to keep the program going as we prepared to leave.

Once again, we found Spectrum's most profound effect among the teachers, as a lens in helping them see all their students as talented individuals with the potential to learn and grow. As O'Brien noted in her final interview,

> I'll never look at children the same way again . . . it's an eye-opener for me because I never perceived children as being more than math and English and reading . . . I never thought that they had the mechanical ability or movement ability or music ability that was exhibited here in the classroom.

Furthermore, said the principal, Connections convinced her that these abilities are indeed intelligences, not frills. "It has been very embedded in me that unless the children are showing evidence of highly developed logical-mathematical and liguistic intelligences, then they're not as intelligent as other children. And I saw graphically that that just is not the case."

The teachers also noted the importance of giving children time to experiment with different concepts and materials. They planned to make concerted efforts to put more time in their schedule for open-ended, "messing about" across domains. O'Brien said that, having seen children's strengths in and strong attractions to different activities emerge, she could never set up her classroom without the storytelling and take-apart centers again.

Particularly compelling to the teachers in terms of influencing their practice and thinking was the act of observing children closely, with an emphasis on identifying areas of strength or interest. Stith and O'Brien remarked that a rich classroom environment must be in place before worthwhile observations can occur. Both teachers changed their classrooms to accomodate changes in instructional practice: they set up learning centers on an ongoing part-time basis, made room to display children's work, and changed the configurations to allow for cooperative, small-group work.

Challenges of Domain-Based Mentorships

Thus far, a reader might question whether there is any reason *not* to conduct a mentorship program such as Connections. Given the benefits and joy that the program engendered, we would enthusiastically encourage and support a similar effort. However, it was not easy nor without its problems. One of the most troubling and complicating aspects of the program was the regular absences of three mentors.

One mentor did not come for 5 weeks in a row and was virtually replaced by a Spectrum staff member. Another missed three sessions in a row, leading several children to ask if he would ever return. Although Spectrum staff members and the teachers filled in for the missing mentors, we were not practitioners in the domain, as the mentors were. Moreover, we were less "special," more familiar faces to the students than were their mentors. Nor did our presence undo the fact that their mentors obviously had failed to show up.

Clearly, these absenses suggest that in terms of conducting such a program, the importance of mentors' commitment, responsibility, and accountability must be presented unequivocally. The message must be clear that showing up every week is the most important aspect of the program and that deciding not to sign on is preferable to checkered attendance. The program can be designed so that individuals who cannot make a weekly commitment can make one-time or occasional visits to the classroom as special guests.

Another challenging aspect of the program was the emphasis on the mentor as domain expert, or teacher. We anticipated that asking nonteachers to step into a weekly teaching role would prove difficult, and therefore we built in supports throughout the program. Training session activities, weekly phone conversations, activity and instructional suggestions were all a part of the support structure. Our work helping mentors create and organize appropriate and meaningful projects was especially important. Still, for some mentors, being a teacher for an hour a week was a great challenge.

These two major concerns, mentor absenses and mentors as teachers, have implications for training sessions. Our training sessions were a key element in building team cohesion among the mentors, introducing the students and school, and sharing important information regarding children's behavior and child development. If we could do it over again, however, we would emphasize the time commitment more, and more seriously. We would make the agreement about weekly attendance more formal, perhaps through written understandings. And the focus of every meeting would be teaching.

As every good teacher knows, an individual cannot simply step into a classroom and teach well. It is unclear to what extent more, or more intensive, training would have helped the mentors, given the limited time period of the program. However, we do know that a more concerted effort could have been made to prepare mentors to teach young children.

Overall, a program such as Connections requires a set of committed adults: mentors, teachers, and, we suggest, a coordinator. The support and coordinating role that Spectrum researchers played for Connections was critical to the functioning of the mentorship program. Finding, screening, training, and supporting mentors, being a liaison between school and community, and assisting with implementation of field trips and special events are time-consuming activities. A designated program coordinator is essential to the establishment of any program such as Connections.

A Culminating Connection

Individuals who had contributed their hearts and minds to the Connections Project—mentors, teachers, parents, Spectrum researchers, and of course the children—came together to share and celebrate their accomplishments at the end of the school year. Each mentor group proudly, and sometimes shyly, shared their newfound understandings and the products they had created over the past few months.

Jackson's group displayed essays created from photographs they shot and developed, taken with cameras they had made themselves. They talked about the trials and tribulations of mastering both the technical and artistic components of photography. Reid's group performed a song-and-dance routine, using chimes made of keys and other instruments they had crafted themselves. The video artists presented their video, a display of abilities in dance, song, visual arts, and production techniques.

The athlete groups shared a video presentation of the "mini-Olympics" that they had designed and successfully conducted for both classrooms. The urban planner groups exhibited the models of "favorite places" they had fashioned, including an art museum/school, a classroom, a mentor's office, and a circus, while they comfortably discussed issues of scale, design, and construction.

As we watched, we recalled that during preproject interviews many of these children had expressed television-inspired career goals, including "fireman" and "policeman," even "Superman." Now "photographer," "video maker," and "designer" supplanted those aspirations.

Keisha said that she wanted to be a "video maker . . . cause you can make all kinds of movies. . . . You can let children use [a video camera] if you go to their school." Juan wanted to be a photographer because "you get to take pictures of the rocks and the yard and you don't have to worry that [they] might not come out . . . because you know how to do it." James, on the urban planner team, said he wanted to be an artist. His mother commented,

> He took a liking to art and design work. He brought the model of the classroom home and talked about it, talked about why he designed it that way, talked about the mentor, and the tools, and about the trip. . . . He has identified something unique and different from what most kids see about jobs and work.

We were gratified with children's changes in career goals, but not because they had changed their minds about what they wanted to be and would now fill the world's ranks of photographers, musicians, and urban planners. We were delighted because it was clear that children had seen and *experienced* new and very real possibilities for themselves, beyond vague or unrealistic television stereotypes. With the friendship and support of their mentors, working with real tools of the trade, the students came to recognize their own abilities and interests, and that these very abilities and interests could enable them as adults to make real and important contributions to the world.

Now on this final day of Spectrum Connections, the "connections" to which we had aspired were clear: connections between child and mentor, and between school and community. For the children, there were connections between themselves, something and someone they loved, and life beyond school walls.

A powerful note upon which to end, the Connections Project represented the last phase of the Spectrum research. Not that we believed that all of our questions were answered, nor that we had done all there was to do in terms of understanding and applying the Spectrum approach. But as an organization, Project Zero was moving in a different direction, toward working with whole schools and school districts. In order for our understanding of teaching and classroom practice to grow, we could no longer work in relative isolation, with individual teachers, in individual classrooms. That meant going beyond the implementation of Spectrum and MI theory in isolation, to exploring how it fits with other ideas that are important in the broader picture of school reform. The lessons we had learned in Spectrum became an important element of the portfolio we brought to new collaborations, such as Communities for Authentic Teaching, Learning, and Assessment for all Students (ATLAS), an attempt to design model school programs extending from kindergarten through high school.

Fortunately, though we at Project Zero have taken a backseat, the work on Spectrum goes forward. Today, it is led by individuals in the best position to ask questions and seek answers: practitioners in classrooms around the country.

REFERENCES

Abell Foundation, Inc. (1989a). *Mentoring manual: A guide to program development and implementation.* Author: Baltimore, MD.

Abell Foundation, Inc. (1989b). *The two of us: A handbook for mentors.* Author: Baltimore, MD.

Comer, J. P. (1980). *School power.* New York: Free Press.

Damon, W. (1990). Reconciling the literacies of generations. *Daedalus, 119*(2), 115–140.

Gardner, H. (1991). *The unschooled mind.* New York: Basic Books.

Gray, J., & Viens, J. (1994, Winter). The theory of multiple intelligences: Understanding cognitive diversity in school. In *National Forum, 74*(1), 22–25.

Heath, S. B. (1983). *Ways with words.* New York: Cambridge University Press.

Jacobs, H. H. (1989). *Interdisciplinary curriculum design: Design and implementation.* Alexandria, VA: Association for Supervision and Curriculum Development.

Katz, L., & Chard, S. (1989). *Engaging children's minds: The project approach.* Norwood, NJ: Ablex.

Kozol, J. (1991). *Savage inequalities.* New York: Crown.

Zimilies, H. (1987). The Bank Street approach. In J. L. Roopnarine & E. Johnson (Eds.), *Approaches to early childhood education.* (pp. 163–178). Columbus, OH: Merrill.

CHAPTER 6

THE MANY FACES OF SPECTRUM

In Gloucester, Massachusetts, elementary teachers revamp their curriculum to help children become independent learners who solve open-ended problems in a wide range of disciplines. In Montgomery County, Maryland, a prekindergarten-through-second-grade-school with a multicultural population develops a new definition of gifted and talented to include children with nonverbal skills. In Shoreham-Wading River, Long Island, the teachers at a kindergarten–grade-1 school gain a newfound respect for at-risk students when they look for areas of strength and use them to improve the students' learning opportunities. Outside of Seattle, Washington, a teacher in a grade 3–5, multiage classroom inspires a new enthusiasm for learning in his students when he incorporates all the intelligences into his lesson plans.

These are just a few examples of the ways that teachers and administrators have applied the Spectrum approach to their schools or classrooms. But unlike the projects we have discussed in previous chapters, these efforts were not initiated by Spectrum. Instead, practitioners heard or read about the research and started making changes on their own, with only minimal consultation with Spectrum staff.

Based on inquiries to our office and information we have received at conferences and school visits, we estimate that more than 200 schools and classrooms across the country are attempting to put into practice an approach that incorporates MI theory and the Spectrum model of implementation (Harvard Project Zero, 1995). None of these sites are Spectrum sites; they are public and private schools and teachers with dreams and problems similar to those of thousands of other schools and teachers across the country. Nor are they all implementing the Spectrum model in the same way.

Today, Project Zero is trying to expand the outreach services it offers in support of schools. We have developed an Internet-based network, available by subscription, providing a newsletter and an interactive discussion forum so that educators can share ideas about thinking, learning, and related topics. We are also collecting data from schools around the country to identify those practices associated with effective implementation of MI theory.

In this chapter we will examine four sites and the different ways they have adapted Spectrum ideas to address specific problems or to enrich their educational program. We will conclude by using their experiences to arrive at some general conclusions about the factors most conducive to a successful implementation of the Spectrum approach.

BRUCE CAMPBELL: REVAMPING CURRICULUM TO HELP ALL CHILDREN SUCCEED

In general, we believe that the Spectrum approach works best when implemented in a collaborative fashion—by a group of teachers at a school, by a whole school, and someday, we hope, by a whole school system. But there are cases where an individual, single-handedly, has been able to make measurable differences in student learning. One of these individuals is teacher and consultant Bruce Campbell, who used MI theory to transform the way he presented curriculum in his multiage third-to-fifth-grade classroom in the Marysville School District outside of Seattle, Washington. Change would have come more easily and completely if he could have joined forces with his colleagues, he says. But at the time, the principal and other faculty members in his building were not interested in a new approach, and he simply could not wait to change their minds.

Learning Centers and Projects

Campbell read Gardner's *Frames of Mind* in the mid-1980s, then heard him speak at a conference in Tarrytown, New York. Gardner's words struck a chord. Perhaps Campbell's most unresponsive students were not distracted, or stubborn, or even learning disabled. Perhaps they just needed to learn in different ways.

"Thursday night I was sitting in bed and had a vision of my classroom with seven different learning centers," says Campbell. "The next day I discussed it with my students and principal, and over the weekend I went in to school and redid my classroom. My first trial efforts began Monday morning."

Campbell retained his approach of using thematic instructional units, but tried to present each major idea in ways that reflected the seven intelligences. He began each day with a 15-minute lesson presenting the central ideas to be explored. Students, working in groups that stayed together for about a month, then spent 2 or 3 hours circulating through seven different learning centers, performing activities that approached the lesson from many different entry points.

For a unit on photosynthesis, students might read or write a description of photosynthesis (linguistic intelligence); use watercolors to paint a picture of the process (visual); create a song or rhythm pattern representing the steps involved in photosynthesis (musical); create a chart or timeline of the steps involved in photosynthesis (mathematical); perform a dance or movement sequence representing photosynthesis (bodily-kinesthetic); meet in small groups to discuss the role of chloroplasts in photosynthesis and draw parallels to the process of change in their own lives (interpersonal); and write a journal entry that reflects on a personally transformative experience and compare it to photosynthesis (intrapersonal) (Campbell, Campbell, & Dickinson, 1996). Afterward, students would meet as a group to share the song, dances, models, or other work they had produced.

"Initially, I was doing some trivial activities that were hands on, interactive, and fun, but not necessarily meaningful," he commented. Over time, he was able to develop learning exercises that did a better job of advancing students' understanding of the topic. For example, children who are drawing a diagram of a grasshopper might be asked to consider how the shape of its mouth and legs relates to the food it eats and the way it moves.

In Campbell's classroom, students spent the afternoon working on projects; they had free reign to select the topic and the format (model, play, song, story, game, etc.) in which they would present their findings. They might spend 3 or 4 weeks conducting research and preparing to make a presentation to the class. The act of public performance was a valuable element of these projects, for it required children to demonstrate an understanding of the topic at hand, lent an air of importance to the work, and developed social and language skills they will need throughout their working lives.

"While the learning centers are structured and teacher directed, projects are student-centered, self-directed, and open-ended," Campbell explains. "The students get to make a lot of choices for themselves, so they are very motivated. I see them working in their areas of strength, using the skills they acquired in the learning centers."

Changes in Social Dynamics

By helping students develop their own strategies for learning, Campbell has been able to reach students who might otherwise be pulled out of the classroom for special education. By valuing and recognizing their areas of strength, he says, teachers also can change the way in which these children are perceived by their peers. MI provides a way to shake up the traditional social hierarchy in the classroom, creating situations in which different children can take the lead. Children with verbal and mathematical skills are not the only ones perceived as high achievers; musicians, artists, and negotiators all are highly sought after for collaborative projects that involve posters, graphs, skits, songs, models, and other types of presentations.

Campbell tells the story of Richard, a special education student who in the third grade still could barely read. One day, a classmate ran up to Campbell and told him to go to the music learning center. Richard was conducting his classmates as they performed a complex three-part rhythm piece he had just composed, a piece far more complex than even his teacher could have created. Each day brought new evidence of Richard's musical gift, a talent that had never been noticed by his parents or teachers. He began to make friends and by the end of the year had formed his own band.

Within a month, continues Campbell, Richard was reading chapter books, his foot tapping and his body swaying. There could be many reasons for Richard's progress: a boost in confidence and self-esteem; higher expectations on the part of teachers; a feeling of acceptance by classmates that enabled Richard to take new risks; or just plain coincidence. But Campbell favors another explanation: that Richard learned how to use his area of strength—his sense of rhythm—to master an area of challenge.

There is no doubt that MI has helped Campbell see children such as Richard in a new light. "I think *everybody* can be successful academically and show academic improvement," he says. Indeed, Campbell reports in an article in *Childhood Education* (Campbell, 1992), every child he taught during the first 4 years of his MI program was able to find an area of success.

Campbell also reported other favorable learning outcomes. Students who previously had been labeled as having behavior problems showed rapid improvement during the first 6 weeks of school, began making contributions to their groups, and by year's end were assuming constructive leadership roles. Students assumed more responsibility for their own learning, both as members of cooperative groups during center time and as self-starters for their individual research projects. Some children reported that they enjoyed school for the first time. And academic achievement improved as measured by both classroom and standardized tests; California Achievement Test scores for the 1988–89 class, for example, were above district and state averages in all areas (Campbell, 1992). When CAT scores for Campbell's classroom remained above average year after year, the skeptical principal became Campbell's strongest supporter.

In addition, applying MI theory led to Campbell's own growth as a teacher. He saw his role change from that of director to facilitator as students became more involved in the process of discovery and more vocal about the subjects they wished to explore. Particularly in the first few years, he found it challenging to plan activities in those disciplines he was not used to teaching. He began to enlist the aid of the art, music, and physical education teachers in his search for subject expertise. This kind of collaboration can happen naturally when a whole school embraces an MI approach, and benefits students and teachers alike.

Campbell has spent many years refining his personal approach to establishing an MI classroom. He has published books and videos on the subject and serves as a consultant in his own and other school districts. His own preference is to try to incorporate the seven intelligences in every lesson, to ensure that the material he is presenting is accessible to every student in his class. Furthermore, performing an activity using different intelligences forces students to apply information in new contexts, a process that deepens their understanding of the topic.

It is important to repeat, however, that multiple intelligences should not be invoked for their own sake, but to advance well thought-out educational goals. The learning center approach, used in Campbell's and the Somerville classrooms, is only one way of implementing Spectrum or MI theory. At Project Zero, for example, researchers have become increasingly interested in ways that multiple intelligences can be recruited to help students attain a deep understanding of pivotal ideas (Gardner, in press). At the high school level, topics could include "evolution" or "the Holocaust"; at the elementary level, "community" or "the water cycle." Multiple intelligences would be recruited as students grappled with the topics from different perspectives and demonstrated their understanding in a variety of ways, rather than to meet a daily quota.

In the pages that follow, we will offer examples of sites that have implemented MI theory using a theme-based or project approach. We also will see what happens when teachers work together across grades or even across an entire school.

FULLER SCHOOL: NEW ASSESSMENTS DRIVE CURRICULUM CHANGE

At the Fuller School in Gloucester, Massachusetts, teachers volunteer to participate in a "school within a school" where MI is practiced. The Fuller School is a kindergarten–grade-5 elementary, with 10 self-contained classes for students with serious mental or physical disabilities. Altogether the school serves about 800 students, with a staff of about 70 teachers and 20 paraprofessionals.

Located about 45 minutes north of Boston, Gloucester is a picturesque harbor community that has been severely affected by recent federal bans on fishing, enacted to protect overfished species from extinction. Residents include an economic mix of lawyers, doctors, and teachers as well as fishermen and laborers at a local fish processing plant. Many children at Fuller come from economically disadvantaged families. Although nearly all the students are White, the student body is ethnically diverse, with a significant number of first-generation Portuguese and Sicilian immigrants who speak languages other than English at home (about 8% of the town's students speak English as a second language).

The impetus for adopting an MI/Spectrum approach at the Fuller School came from William Leary, the former district superintendent. Dr. Leary became interested in MI during the late 1980s because it offered a theoretical framework to support his belief that all children should find a way to succeed and that education should offer them opportunities to pursue their interests and develop their talents to the maximum. The Fuller School was selected for the pilot program because of the quality of the school's faculty and the enthusiasm of Ron Eckel, then principal. Like Dr. Leary, many Fuller teachers and administrators felt that MI theory was consistent with their existing beliefs and practices.

Assessments Shed Light on Curriculum as well as Students

Fuller's pilot MI program began at the kindergarten level. As the first step, a team of three kindergarten teachers and two special education teachers began meeting to develop ways to implement the Spectrum assessments. In early 1990, the team members participated in a 2-day in-service training workshop at Project Spectrum, learning to use the Modified Spectrum Field Inventory (MSPFI). MSPFI is a shortened version of the Spectrum assessment instrument used at the Eliot-Pearson Children's School (described in Chapter 2) and is intended to measure diverse cognitive abilities in kindergarten and first-grade rather than preschool children.

Implemented the following September, the assessment process did indeed help the MI team members paint a more detailed, complete picture of individual children. But, according to one kindergarten teacher, it also raised a significant question: "Why were some children terrified when they were asked to answer an open-ended question or solve a problem?" After a series of discussions, the team members decided that the children's consternation reflected a weakness in the curriculum. "Our curriculum has never asked our children to solve any serious, life-related problems," another teacher commented. "Our curriculum is to make one like mine, do it like this. If we don't change our curriculum, we will not see changes in our children."

Over the next few years, teachers in the model program worked on curriculum development—designing, implementing, revising, and trying again—keeping MI theory as a focus. After years of experimenting, the Fuller MI teachers concluded that a Spectrum curriculum must have the following three features: (a) it covers many areas of learning, and basic skills are taught in a context meaningful to children; (b) it is process oriented and activity based and can be implemented in a variety of ways or combined with a variety of instructional strategies, such as thematic units, projects, and learning centers; and (c) it involves many different ways of assessing children's knowing and doing in a wide range of areas (Fuller School, 1995a).

Working with MI prompted teachers to take a fresh look not just at curriculum but at almost all aspects of their practice, from classroom organization to assessment strategies (see Figure 6.1). At the kindergarten level, for example, the three teachers worked together to plan thematic units that would draw on all the different intelligences. They taught the units as a team. Each teacher took responsibility for presenting the unit in terms of two intelligences, with the linguistic intelligence embedded throughout. Two days a week, the children spent a half hour in each of the other two teachers' rooms.

For a unit on elections, one teacher helped the children learn about the political process by thinking about what points to include in campaign songs for imaginary candidates (a fox, a beaver, and a bear); another teacher encouraged the children to create campaign posters and papier-mâché models of the candidates. Children also made up campaign slogans and speeches, activities that required them to learn about the characteristics of the different animals as well as to sharpen their language skills. After marking ballots for the candidate of their choice, the children tabulated and graphed the results as an exercise in math.

Like Bruce Campbell, the Fuller School teachers tried to find ways to help children take responsibility for their own learning. When launching a new unit, they often asked students to suggest activities that would explore the topic using multiple intelligences. This process not only made the curriculum meaningful to the student, but also gave teachers a sense of what children knew about the topic before formal study began. During one site visit, Spectrum staff watched first and second graders work together in small groups to brainstorm activities for a unit on friendship.

Just as new methods of assessing student ability prompted curriculum reform, the change of curriculum, in turn, prompted teachers to consider

FIGURE 6.1. What's a Natural Course for MI Teachers? [Adapted from Fuller School. (1994). *What's a Natural Course for MI Teachers.* Gloucester, MA: Gloucester Public Schools. © 1994 Multiple Intelligences Program, Gloucester Public Schools]

STEP 1 Students are engaged in teacher-directed activities. These often rely on preexisting methodologies and guidelines such as Whole Language, Won Way, Writing Process, Math Their Way, AIMS, and established math and reading series, including Dalcroze and Orff.

STEP 2 The teacher begins to see learning less in terms of discrete skills and more as a developmental continuum. Concepts are integrated into activities to accommodate the broad range of learners' needs, building upon methodologies suggested in Step 1.

STEP 3 The teacher begins to structure learning around MI theory. This often includes cooperative learning strategies focusing on the classroom as a community of learners. Teachers begin to rely on one another for sharing ideas and to collaborate around instruction recognizing different strengths and styles in teaching. This holds true for both specialists and classroom teachers.

STEP 4 The teacher begins to use photos, journals, videotapes, portfolios, audiotapes, and surveys to document MI activities. The teacher experiences "aha" moments as he or she recognizes learning in intelligence areas. The teacher often shares this increased awareness with colleagues. Teachers value the unique process of learning exhibited by each child through the intelligences.

STEP 5 Learning becomes more student centered. The teacher assists children in becoming more autonomous. Students become aware of their own learning process and independently experience their own "aha" moments in intelligence areas. Teachers examine developmentally appropriate expectations and curriculum with greater intensity.

STEP 6 The teacher deepens his or her understanding of options in both learning and assessment strategies. The teacher broadens documentation practices to include more individualized assessment. This may begin with one specific intelligence area and is supported by collaboration with specialists and other colleagues. This is a reciprocal process in which specialists can now rely on classroom teachers for documentation and assessment.

STEP 7 The teacher begins to take a more active role in the decision-making process of the program via participation in team or whole-group activities. This may emerge at varying stages as outlined in the steps above.

new ways of assessing what students had learned. With the help of Steven Seidel, a researcher at Project Zero, the Gloucester teachers developed a process to help students reflect upon their work (Fuller School, 1996).

In a special publication about the Fuller MI program, called *Hands on,* fifth-grade teacher Cherylann Parker gave an example of the assessment process at work (Parker, 1995). Her class had just completed a study of the Civil War as part of the social studies curriculum. After two students, Margaret and Alicia, performed a poem and dance they had created, a student facilitator asked them to reflect upon their work using questions the class had developed earlier. "What were the easiest parts of this project and why?" he asked. "What were some of the hardest parts and why?" "What part of the project are you most proud of and why?" "What part do you feel was not your best effort?" "What do you need to do next time to make sure you produce a better project?"

The facilitator then turned to the audience, asking classmates to point out the most successful elements of the work and make constructive suggestions for possible improvements. In order to answer the questions and evaluate one another's projects, students had to think carefully about just what it is that makes for "good" work.

The Fuller teachers continued working to develop assessment measures that reflected a full range of student strengths. They sought instruments that could give a more complete picture of the ways that children were achieving curricular goals, including the child's level of engagement, interest, and acquisition of skills and knowledge in different learning areas. To this end they developed a multiple intelligences report card, instituted student portfolios and criteria for evaluating them, and encouraged the collaborative assessment process described above. In addition to reflecting the individuality of students' achievements, these instruments provided useful information for determining subsequent curriculum objectives and evaluating the teachers's instructional methods.

Collaboration and Reflection: Keys to Success

As in making any innovation, to adopt the Spectrum approach is to embark on an uncharted journey, full of twists and turns. The Fuller story is no exception. While MI staff members worked hard to change and improve their curriculum content and instructional strategies, the program attracted great attention from the public. Newspaper reporters, television camera crews, and visitors from various parts of the country often could be seen brushing past students in the corridor.

The attention that the MI program received, although exhilarating, also created tension between MI and non-MI teachers in the school. Except at the kindergarten level, each grade has been composed of both

MI and non-MI classrooms (in July 1997, all first-grade staff voluntarily joined the MI team). "Sure, they [MI teachers] are special," a non-MI teacher voiced her discomfort. "Look, those visitors came here. They passed by my classroom and zoomed into the MI classroom next door as if my students deserve no attention and my students' work merits no praise." Other faculty members seemed to misunderstand the MI program and how it provides alternate ways to help children master essential skills. "This is just another fad," a teacher exclaimed. "Who has time for that? We've got a room full of first graders who need to learn their ABCs."

Personnel changes have posed another serious challenge to the Fuller MI program. The district superintendent, the school principal, and the assistant principal all left in 1993, only 3 years after the MI program was instituted. The departure of these leaders had significant impact because they had been great supporters of the program since its inception. Also, the Fuller MI team changes annually; there can be as many as four new teachers out of 14 classrooms in one year. Although new faculty members bring fresh ideas, they also need a great deal of training and practice in order to become familiar with the program philosophy and feel comfortable about implementing it. Such training and practice take time and often slow down the program's progress.

How does the Fuller MI team face the challenges and solve the problems that inevitably arise? "We have a powerful tool: the ongoing discussions, reflections, and collaborations among all staff members," said Bill Bruns, formerly the MI program coordinator and now a middle-school music teacher and educational consultant in the Philadelphia area. The Fuller MI teachers have seen themselves as pioneers in adapting the MI/Spectrum approach to their own community, developing strategies and procedures as the need arises. MI team members use meeting times (e.g., a weekly grade-level meeting, special-topic meetings, and the annual program retreat) to put their heads together and create a model that best fits the Fuller culture. The weekly faculty meetings serve not only as a workshop for sharing effective instructional strategies and curriculum ideas, but also as a safe environment in which teachers can take risks, experiment with alternative approaches, and critique their own and colleagues' work.

By 1998, the MI program at Fuller School had been operating for 8 years. Initiated with three kindergarten teachers and about 70 children, the program had grown to serve approximately 400 students—about half the student population—in 16 classrooms from kindergarten to grade 5. Comments made to visiting Spectrum staff members reveal enthusiasm about the MI program:

- "The teacher just doesn't throw paper on your desks and tells [sic] you to do it. The games and projects make you want to learn more."

- "We think a lot. We have thinking homework. Like we have to make up a game."
- "We have partners. We help each other in the project."
- "If some kids have trouble with their work, we work together so no one gets left behind."
- "We learn to have fun while we work."

The results of a recent school administration survey of parents with children in the MI program indicate that the parents overwhelmingly support the program and want to continue it (Fuller School, 1995b). Ninety-two percent of those who responded indicated that their children had a successful year. Ninety-six percent said that their children enjoyed the program. Eighty-two percent said that their children acquired essential grade-level skills. Finally, 80% said that their children had developed a better sense of problem solving since entering the MI program.

Despite their increased enthusiasm for learning, the Fuller MI students did not score significantly higher on standardized tests than did the non-MI students during the first few years of the program. This result is not surprising to the Fuller MI staff, because standardized tests are not designed to measure many of the end products of the MI approach to learning, such as confidence, cooperation, self-expression, and critical and creative thinking. To see whether any long-term effects can be detected, Gloucester administrators plan to examine the academic performance of the first cohort of MI students, now attending middle school.

MONTGOMERY KNOLLS ELEMENTARY SCHOOL: DIVERSITY IN GIFTEDNESS

Montgomery Knolls Elementary School, located in Silver Spring, Maryland, is a preschool-through-grade-2 magnet school administered by the Montgomery County Public School system. Offering a Head Start and a preschool program for children with multiple disabilities, the school serves approximately 380 students with a staff of 26 classroom teachers and 20 additional supporting staff.

The school's student population includes those who live in low-income housing or apartments as well as those from middle-class, professional families. During the 1995–96 school year, 48% of the students received free or reduced-price lunch, and 9% spoke English as a second language. Minority enrollment equaled 72%, with 39% of the students being African American, 19% Hispanic, and 13% Asian.

In 1990 and then again in 1992, the Montgomery County Public

Schools received 3-year grants under the Jacob K. Javits Gifted and Talented Students Education Program. The Javits program was designed to identify gifted and talented young students who would not normally be identified through traditional assessment methods because their strengths might be masked by economic disadvantage, limited English ability, or developmental differences that might lead to learning disabilities.

Under this program, the county awarded funds to Montgomery Knolls Elementary School to develop an "Early Childhood Gifted Model Program" because of the school's progressive educational practices, including a project-based approach, learning centers, and an emphasis on the development of the whole child. The program administrators chose MI as a guiding theory because it provided psychological and neurological data supporting the premise that children can be intelligent in many different ways. They chose Spectrum as an initial model for implementation because it offered examples of intelligence-fair assessment instruments in diverse domains.

Unlike in the Fuller MI program, which is a school within a school, all of the teachers at Montgomery Knolls were expected to apply MI/Spectrum ideas to their classroom practice. In addition, all of the students in the school were included in the program. The teachers at Montgomery Knolls felt that they did not yet have a clear enough picture of what criteria to use, and in which areas, to decide which students were gifted and talented. Furthermore, they wanted to provide rich experiences to all of their students and learn about the different strengths and potentials that each one of them possessed.

A New Definition of Giftedness

The first question that challenged the Montgomery Knolls staff was how to define giftedness. As we discussed in Chapter 1 of this book, educators traditionally have equated intelligence or "giftedness" with performance on intelligence tests, which tend to focus on students' linguistic and logical-mathematical abilities. Indeed, in the early 1990s Montgomery County also used formal testing to select gifted students, who then became eligible for a variety of special schools and programs.

The Montgomery Knolls teachers were concerned that certain groups of students might be underidentified for gifted education services because of cultural and linguistic barriers. After a series of discussions, the staff issued the following statement: "Cultural values and linguistic differences do not, and should not, determine whether or not an individual is gifted. Rather, they can influence the specific ways in which giftedness is expressed. We need to honor, value, and celebrate the cultural and linguistic diversity of our students, and to do so, we need to find alternative assessment strategies to recognize diversity in giftedness."

With funds provided by the Javits grant, two program specialists had been hired to design and implement the new assessment instruments. These program specialists had read about Project Spectrum and used it as a model for their own work. In 1991, with the help of Spectrum staff, they conducted a series of training workshops at the school. The training influenced the initial development of the Early Childhood Gifted Program in at least two ways. First, domain-specific observations became a common practice for many teachers. "Instead of saying this child is good or problematic in general terms," said kindergarten teacher Karen Bulman, "we now look at the child's performance in specific areas, and we often find out that a child can be excellent in one area, average in another, and rather weak in a third area." Domain-specific observations helped teachers to better understand their students and their particular strengths and weaknesses.

Second, the program specialists used several Spectrum assessment activities—such as the Bus Game (involving mental computation), Assembly (the activity described in Chapter 2, requiring children to take apart and reassemble a food grinder), and Classroom Model (a social understanding activity encouraging children to describe what happens in the classroom)—to answer questions or confirm suspicions arising from observations that they had made of individual children.

Teachers began to see everyday events as opportunities for learning more about their students. For example, Carol Hylton, formerly a second-grade teacher at the school (now a teacher-trainer with the county's Title I program), reported that when the pencil sharpener jammed she took a chance and asked if anyone would like to try to fix it. Chuck, a recent immigrant who spoke little English, confidently took on the task and was able to unjam the machine quickly. To follow up on Hylton's observation, a program specialist conducted a modified version of the Spectrum Assembly Activity with Chuck. Both she and Hylton were astounded by Chuck's facility at taking apart and putting the food grinder back together. "I can't believe an old grinder can give me so much insight into a child!" she announced at a faculty meeting.

Many other insights were gained by using Spectrum tasks that the Montgomery Knolls staff modified to better serve the school's diverse student population. Lupe, a second grader, had not attained a high math score on an intelligence test when she applied to a gifted program at another school. However, at Montgomery Knolls, she answered each question properly on a revised Spanish version of the Bus Game and demonstrated a clear understanding of rather complex math concepts during the game. She was bilingual and had not fully mastered English. Her teachers concluded that the language barrier, not math understanding, had inhibited her performance on the intelligence test. They helped her improve her English skills so that a year later she could be placed in gifted classes.

Eileen, another second grader, had some difficulty in math, but was skillful in painting, drawing, and assembly, and had strong social skills. For example, when a class project required each student to create a patch for a quilt, she assisted others even to the detriment of her own product. Eileen was supportive and helpful to her peers whenever possible and, in turn, always got help when she needed it. She was keenly aware of whom she could ask for help in the classroom, and her performance on the Classroom Model activity confirmed her exceptional ability to understand herself and others. The teacher included this information in Eileen's "Insight Card," an index card on which teachers documented events they observed that revealed something significant about a student, including his or her interaction with materials and people. These Insight Cards were placed in the child's portfolio and used for parent conferences and curriculum planning.

Ironically, the more excited teachers became about their students' nonverbal skills, the more motivated they became to help students overcome language-related deficiencies. They wanted to prepare the children for encounters with teachers at other schools, who might not be as experienced in recognizing nonverbal strengths. For example, a child's musical abilities might be more readily apparent if she also had the communication skills to tell the teacher, "Listen to the tune I made up!"

The Montgomery Knolls teachers began to build linguistic links into—or around—each MI exploratory activity. In kindergarten, for example, teachers set aside the last 15 to 25 minutes of each exploratory period for children to reflect upon and talk about what they accomplished that day. In the first and second grades, children were often asked to share their work verbally, respond to teachers' questions, or create a poem, journal, or other written document. A strong effort was made to help children express their thoughts, feelings, or actions in verbal and written forms, using work in nonverbal domains as the focal point.

Assessment in Context

More than 8 years has passed since the inception of the Montgomery Knolls Early Childhood Gifted Model Program in 1990. Today, the Javits grant no longer exists, but the program's initial goal of identifying and nurturing children's diverse strengths has become part of the school culture. For example, the staff developed an "Observational Checklist for Identifying Learning Strengths," based on the seven intelligences (see Figure 6.2). Classroom teachers complete it for each child twice a year,

FIGURE 6.2. Observational Checklist for Multiple Intelligences [Source: Montgomery Knolls Elementary School, Montgomery County Public Schools]

Child's Name _____ Teacher _____ Grade _____

done by 2nd Fri. in Nov.	done by the end of May		
		Linguistic	
_____	_____	1.	Chooses to memorize poems, songs, stories
_____	_____	2.	Starts conversations or discussions on his/her own
_____	_____	3.	Expresses ideas easily orally _____ in writing
_____			
_____	_____	4.	Describes an object or idea in several ways
_____	_____	5.	Readily verbalizes background knowledge and factual information
_____	_____	6.	Asks many questions
_____	_____	7.	Shows verbal ability in English, considering another language is used in the home
_____	_____	8.	Enjoys reading books
_____	_____	9.	Uses advanced vocabulary

		Logical/Mathematical	
_____	_____	1.	Easily communicates mathematical thinking when problem solving
_____	_____	2.	Computes number problems in his or her head
_____	_____	3.	Constructs a strategy for solving a problem
_____	_____	4.	Is able to plan or describe steps or events in order
_____	_____	5.	Sorts and classifies objects or pictures
_____	_____	6.	Assembles puzzles with skill and enjoyment
_____	_____	7.	Displays skill in computer usage
_____	_____	8.	Asks questions about how things work

		Intrapersonal	
_____	_____	1.	Self-motivated ___; independent ___; resourceful__
_____	_____	2.	Self-confident
_____	_____	3.	Expresses how he or she is feeling
_____	_____	4.	Has a sense of humor
_____	_____	5.	Can laugh at oneself
_____	_____	6.	Sticks to one's beliefs
_____	_____	7.	Takes risks
_____	_____	8.	Concentrates on topics or tasks
_____	_____	9.	Persistent in self-selected activity
_____	_____	10.	Chooses to work alone
_____	_____	11.	Accepts ownership for own behavior
_____	_____	12.	Has a realistic sense of his or her strengths or weaknesses
_____	_____	13.	Is able to learn from his or her successes and failures
_____	_____	14.	Adds unique qualities to a task (creative)

Interpersonal

_____ _____	1. Eager participant in group activities
_____ _____	2. Enjoys informally teaching others
_____ _____	3. Others seek out his or her company
_____ _____	4. Likes to play games with other children
_____ _____	5. Likes to work in cooperative groups
_____ _____	6. Helps to solve conflicts

Bodily-Kinesthetic

_____ _____	1. Enjoys role playing
_____ _____	2. Enjoys taking things apart and putting them back together
_____ _____	3. Prefers to touch and explore the shape of objects in order to learn about them
_____ _____	4. Enjoys movement activities
_____ _____	5. Has a dramatic way of expressing self
_____ _____	6. Shows good fine motor coordination
_____ _____	7. Shows good gross motor coordination
_____ _____	8. Physically interprets stories, poems, songs

Spatial

_____ _____	1. Puts things together imaginatively to form a construction
_____ _____	2. Shows an understanding of physical perspective
_____ _____	3. Takes things apart and can put them back together
_____ _____	4. Can organize and group objects
_____ _____	5. Carefully plans use of space
_____ _____	6. Includes relevant details in artwork
_____ _____	7. Enjoys puzzles and mazes
_____ _____	8. Acquires more meaning from nonprint materials

Musical

_____ _____	1. Reproduces newly heard melody or rhythm
_____ _____	2. Composes rhythms, patterns, or melodies
_____ _____	3. Creates own words to fit familiar tunes
_____ _____	4. Keeps a beat with musical instruments
_____ _____	5. Sings on key
_____ _____	6. Sings or hums melodically during independent activities
_____ _____	7. Experiments with objects to create different sounds
_____ _____	8. Transforms environmental sounds into musical sounds or compositions
_____ _____	9. Learns basic concepts through music

Comments

in the fall and spring. The fall observations help identify each child's strengths and weaknesses and inform curriculum planning. The spring observations are used in order to evaluate the progress that the child has made over the year as well as to examine the child's current MI profile. If, in fact, the teacher is providing a classroom with an array of possibilities for developing diverse interests and skills, students could show changes in their MI profile over the year.

Although observations of students as they go about classroom activities are the basic tool for teacher assessments, children are involved in the assessment process as well. For example, they fill out a survey in which they are asked to rate themselves in terms of which activities they liked to do and were good at. At the kindergarten level, children use four rating categories ("all of the time," "most of the time," "some of the time," "none of the time") to mark themselves on 22 items, such as "I share my feelings and ideas with others"; "I like to work by myself"; and "I like to work in groups." The information not only helps teachers plan curriculum, but also provides a starting point for student-teacher conferences. At these meetings, the teacher describes the child's strengths and areas of progress during the year; the child is encouraged to add to or disagree with the teacher's comments. Thus, the child is encouraged to see assessment not as a judgment, but as part of the learning process.

Just as in Gloucester, teachers at Montgomery Knolls also began to experiment with portfolio assessment as a means of capturing the diverse ways in which children can demonstrate their learning. Some teachers used audio- and videotape to document particular areas of strength or weakness that they noticed in their students. Others collected students' drawings and written work to supplement classroom observations and to provide documentation of a student's growth over time. The very process of collecting and saving student work increases its importance; instead of being thrown away, the work can be reexamined by teachers and students, in light of all they have learned about themselves and the discipline since the work was produced (Krechevsky & Seidel, 1998).

Portfolio assessment was instituted at Montgomery Knolls under the Javits grant program and later became an integral part of the reading and language arts program. The school has developed its own guidelines for portfolio collection (see Figure 6.3). The children's work is gathered from different sources, including the student's own selection, teacher's suggestions, and items required of all students at the grade level. Portfolios are passed on from grade to grade within Montgomery Knolls and are sometimes sent to the next school that the child attends.

At present, Montgomery County still uses formal testing to select gifted students at the second-grade level and up. Even by this measure, the

FIGURE 6.3. Guidelines for Portfolios [Source: Montgomery Knolls Elementary School, Montgomery County Public Schools]

Kindergarten Portfolio
by Karen Bulman, Lori Skilnick, Mary Margaret Landers, and Letitia Worthington

• MI checklist
• Self-portrait collected three times a year (September, January, June)
• Writing samples collected at least three times a year
• Individual Student Performance Sheet (skills checklist)
• Parent Survey from kindergarten orientation
• Coloring/cutting samples at least three times a year
• Photographs as available
• Any additional materials that show progress, strengths, or both
• Math materials including worksheet follow-ups to hands-on activities for meeting Instructional System in Mathematics objectives (county-wide standards)
• If substitutes can be provided, teachers will meet individually with children to work on self-report cards, goal setting, and portfolio interviews

First-Grade Portfolio
by Barbara Williams, Susie Lively, and Mary Michaels

• Writing samples (literary writing)
• Painting
• Any work that relates to individual strengths
• Peer or parent feedback forms
• Statement of personal goals
• Electronic pieces as it fits the class, selected by children and adults, including scanned samples of writings and drawings expressive writing as it relates to the seven intelligences reflective questionnaire
• Math problem-solving strategies
• Photos of student-designed products
• Evaluation forms (teacher diagnostic tools)
• Self-portraits (collected at beginning, middle, and end of year)

Second-Grade Portfolio
by Patti Jones, Deborah Chapman, and Velma Buckner

• Self-portraits (collected at beginning, middle, and end of year)
• Self-evaluation report cards (collected at beginning, middle, and end of year)
• Writing samples
• Goals
• Logical-mathematical papers
• Action photos
• Insight cards from specialist
• Parent feedback forms

number of Montgomery Knolls students identified as gifted and talented increased during the model program, from 27% of grade-2 students in 1988 to 51% in 1994. This gain indicates that teachers may have found ways to bridge from children's areas of strength to the kind of language and math learning measured on paper-and-pencil tests.[1]

BRIARCLIFF ROAD ELEMENTARY SCHOOL: TUNING IN TO THE DIVERSITY OF LEARNERS

Located in the Shoreham-Wading River School District on Long Island, roughly 80 miles east of New York, Briarcliff Road Elementary School has for many years tried to see its students as individuals with distinct ways of learning. It serves 188 children in kindergarten and first grade and has one preschool classroom for children with special needs. The faculty includes 10 classroom teachers and a number of specialists, including full-time reading, speech, and resource room teachers as well as part-time music, physical education, and art teachers.

The school serves a middle-class and stable community. Many children come from intact families, with parents who work as New York City firefighters, police officers, and teachers as well as scientists at the nearby Brookhaven National Laboratory. The district has a history of commitment to education, and often, schools are viewed as community centers. For example, the public library is housed in the high school, and computers and exercise equipment in the schools are available for public use.

For years, taxes from the Shoreham Nuclear Power Plant enabled the district to purchase computers and other equipment for the schools, to maintain small class sizes, and to provide generous professional development opportunities for teachers. When Spectrum staff members visited Briarcliff in 1992, class size averaged 18 students, and each classroom was outfitted with six computers and two printers. Since then, protests over safety concerns have prevented the power plant from going into operation, and the district has had to increase class sizes to about 22 students and significantly reduce funds for professional development.

The district's commitment to professional development has enabled Briarcliff's teachers and administrators to attend summer institutes, visit innovative programs at schools around the country (including the Key School in Indianapolis, the first school based on MI theory), and invite educational experts to give workshops at their school. For example, during the early 1980s staff members encountered "constructivism," an approach based on Piaget's theories of cognitive development that emphasizes the child's role as an active learner who constructs his or her own understanding of the world based on experience. A dedication to constructivism at Briarcliff led to a project called Cognitive Levels Matching, which was intended to align curriculum with the developmental level of the children. This project in turn led to ongoing professional discussion and reflection on the "child's point of view" in the learning process.

In 1989 Gardner was invited to give a talk at a conference in the Shoreham-Wading River School District. Briarcliff administrators and teachers attended the meeting and found that MI theory fit with the philo-sophical notions that they had been practicing in their school and class-rooms. They were especially intrigued by the scientific evidence for each intelligence and the connection between the intelligences and the differ-ent endstates, or occupations, for which children ultimately were being prepared.

In particular, the Briarcliff teachers wanted to learn more about Spec-trum. They invited three Spectrum researchers to give workshops on two occasions and, in the summer of 1989, to provide a summer course for the entire faculty on MI/Spectrum work and its applications in the Briarcliff School culture. The decision to implement an MI approach to education was achieved through consensus, rather than through an administrative decision; the ideas were integrated into existing classroom practice, rather than instituted as a separate program; and changes were made on a school-wide, rather than individual, basis.

The faculty was particularly interested in two different areas: how to incorporate all the intelligences into a project approach to instruction, which they were developing with the assistance of Sylvia Chard of the University of Alberta in Edmonton, Canada, a leading expert in project-based curriculum; and how to use MI to evaluate and serve children at risk for school failure and learning disabilities.

Integrating Multiple Intelligences Into Projects

The Briarcliff teachers had been taking a thematic approach to instruc-tion; curricular units already included some activities that cut across disci-plines. After being introduced to Gardner's ideas, teachers began to use MI as a framework for designing thematic activities that spanned the seven intelligences. Teachers expanded the units they were accustomed to teaching and integrated new domains and activities where they perceived gaps.

Such an interdisciplinary approach broadened the areas of study, and children were noted to have great fun in their learning. However, several staff members expressed concern that the thematic units, as they were im-plementing them, felt contrived. Nancy Sims, a first-grade teacher, explained, "I think it's important that all my kids get broad experience in my classroom. But in the urgency to make sure there's a music part, a math piece, and a spatial piece, it feels superficial. I think this is taking away from the meaningfulness of the activities and from how in-depth we can get in our units."

Thematic units work well in exploring a topic broadly and widely, and have been used successfully at many schools. But the Briarcliff teachers also were exploring the project-based approach to instruction (Katz & Chard, 1989). They decided to combine the MI and project-based approaches by exploring a single topic in great depth, with different domains, activities, or intelligences invoked as needed in order to answer an important question or to pursue a specific angle. They wanted to encourage children, as a group, to use multiple ways to seek solutions and present results. Thus, children could discover, for themselves, some of the ways that the different intelligences must be exercised to answer questions not just in the classroom, but in the real world.

The project-based approach emphasized the idea that less is more; coverage was considered less important than in-depth study. Instead of treating 15 to 20 themes a year, teachers focused on three to four major projects in combination with discipline-based instruction in basic skills not fully addressed through the projects. They also began planning projects that were driven by important, real-life questions and issues such as elections, pollution, and community life.

A first-grade project on community, for example, enabled teachers to follow up on the interests of students in their class. Meg Scionti's students spent 5 months turning the classroom into a model town, complete with churches, banks, and beach pavilions. They also made pasta at a restaurant owned by one student's parents. Judy Lay's class, in addition to constructing buildings, invited parents to come to school and talk about their work. The children also created firefighters' hats, surveyed other classrooms about what parents did for work, and graphed their results. Nancy Sims's students decided to study their own school as part of the community project. They researched Briarcliff's history, wrote fiction and nonfiction books about the school, investigated its physical structure, explored what was in the basement and drew pictures of what they found, and developed scaled floorplans that allowed them to work on measuring and comparing sizes.

A project on animals was shared throughout the entire school. Children in each class chose an animal to investigate. In one class, children made daily observations of an ant farm, meticulously drawing the tunnels as they studied the different ways that ants contribute to their colonies. They created 3-foot model ants out of papier-mâché, learning about the structure and function of body parts in the process. Children shared information by attending exhibits and "museum" tours in other classes. The children's knowledge about animals was presented in multiple ways, such as exhibits, books, poetry, data collection charts and graphs, pictures, and songs.

Through years of experimentation and practice with projects that integrated MI, the Briarcliff staff came to a better understanding of learning and teaching in three ways. First, they recognized that not all children had to learn the same thing at the same time. During a project, for example, children might be exploring different areas in depth; one child might be constructing an airport while another child was writing a story. In the end, however, the children learned nearly all the material because they spent time sharing, displaying, and critiquing one another's work.

Second, teachers decided that they did not have to teach the entire curriculum through using projects. In order to keep projects authentic, they chose not to force skill lessons into them; therefore, through projects children could acquire many, but not all, the basic skills they needed to learn. The Briarcliff staff felt comfortable with the fact that they would teach some material by direct instruction and other material through project work.

Third, teachers found that MI provided not only an important means of curriculum planning, but also a framework for observing children and reflecting upon their findings. They were also very interested in seeing how MI would help them teach children who were beginning to manifest learning problems.

Bringing the Spectrum Perspective to Assessment of At-Risk Children

Several years before encountering Spectrum, Briarcliff had established a Child Study Team (CST) to evaluate children believed to be at risk for school failure. Such a team, administrators believed, would take a holistic approach to evaluating children who were falling through the cracks. The team included the school psychologist, classroom teachers, the school nurse, special educators, the reading specialist, and the principal. Each member was responsible for one aspect of the child's "core evaluation," be it a developmental history, psychological evaluation, academic testing, or health history. The group would then meet together to discuss the child's developmental profile, brainstorm ways to help the child function better in the classroom, and consider service options for the child.

To a certain degree, the evaluation was quite comprehensive and multidimensional, says Margaret Daugherty, formerly a special education teacher and now Briarcliff's principal. However, the faculty still felt that it was inadequate. Like old wine in new bottles, the evaluation was based on traditional methods of testing and measurement, with heavy emphasis on language and math. Conversation tended to focus on a child's deficits and how they could be "fixed." Multiple intelligence theory confirmed the belief of most of the teachers that children who were considered at risk academically were capable in many other ways. The question was how to identify these areas and enrich these children's learning experience.

The child struggling in school might have a way of knowing and understanding the world that his or her teacher did not see in a classroom setting. The CST set about trying to learn how children with strengths in different areas might process information. Team members wanted to avoid giving more tests to children under review, who already were taking the standard psychological, language, and reading assessments. Instead, they wanted to see if they could develop their own "naturalistic" methods of evaluating and talking about children's strengths. All the team members were asked to develop a model for conducting authentic, or naturalistic, evaluations in their field, and to describe and defend their ideas at group meetings. The art and music specialists were also involved in the process; the art teacher, for example, developed a checklist to identify the hallmarks of spatial thinkers.

The team first used a Spectrum approach to identifying strengths in Robert, a first grader whose older brother had been diagnosed with learning disabilities. Robert was referred to the CST because of language difficulties such as in word retrieval and other learning problems (including difficulty in following instructions and using fine motor skills). He already was receiving speech therapy.

Using the techniques they had developed together, CST members made close observations of Robert as he went about his work. They found that although Robert was easily distracted in large groups, he was in fact a deep, reflective thinker. The reason he often looked lost was that he couldn't change channels until he had completely processed what was going on, said Daugherty. If he was given extra time to answer a question or complete an assignment, he usually could catch up and respond to the teacher's instructions. He was very strong not just intrapersonally, but also interpersonally. A popular child, he always managed to keep the most boisterous children in their place and enjoyed entertaining his classmates with skits.

Through close observations and comparison of their findings, the CST members also learned that Robert possessed a great deal of determination. Once he focused on a task, he would try his best to perform the task well. Art was one example. At the beginning of the school year, Robert could often be found twiddling his pencil, but over time he began to see himself as an artist. With the help of the art specialist and his classroom teacher, he persevered in his drawing and handwriting until these skills really did improve. He even took out books from the library on drawing. At the end of the first grade, he donated a picture he had drawn to the school library, and it is still hanging on the wall.

By capitalizing on Robert's areas of strength, the Briarcliff staff helped him develop confidence in his ability to learn and to contribute to the school community. Today, Robert has finished his elementary school years without being classified as having a learning disability.

Close observation of Robert's pattern of strengths and weaknesses helped teachers gain a better understanding of each intelligence and its manifestations in school activities. Combining their findings with a study of Gardner's book *Frames of Mind*, the teachers discovered for themselves what each intelligence means in a child's daily life and in a classroom setting. The Briarcliff staff is not able to work as intensely with every child who appears at risk as they did with Robert. But the effort to individualize education—to capitalize on each child's strengths in order to prevent learning difficulties down the road—remains an integral part of the school culture. The staff at the Briarcliff School recognizes that the instructional program must have multiple ways in which to present information to children as well as multiple ways for children to share and represent their learning. In this kind of environment, the abilities of at-risk students receive the same respect and appreciation as the abilities traditionally rewarded in schools.

REFLECTIONS ON WORK IN THE FIELD

A school—indeed, a classroom—is a complex system, and in the space of this chapter we could not do justice to the kind of self-examination and risk taking that occurred as teachers adapted a Spectrum or MI approach to their personal or collective efforts at school reform. We hope, however, that these examples have provided some sense of the many different ways that the approach can help schools or teachers work toward their own educational goals. Although there is no single method or pathway applicable to every situation, there are some general patterns that emerge as educators try to adopt an MI/Spectrum approach, and certain elements that appear to be critical for its successful implementation. These elements include studying the theory underlying the reforms; using MI as a means rather than an end; using a collaborative or team approach; and implementing changes that fit school culture.

Studying the Theory

First, to use MI theory appropriately, one must study it and relate it to one's own experience. Educators who are attracted by the MI/Spectrum approach often find that the core ideas are compatible with their own, previously held beliefs. That is, most individuals know from their own experience the wide range of differences that exist between youngsters, and that there are many different forms of success and failure in the world. The MI/Spectrum framework validates these teachers' practical experiences, supports their beliefs, and provides a vocabulary with which to communicate with students, parents, and colleagues.

However, if the MI/Spectrum approach is to succeed in bridging the gap between mere buzzword and internalized teaching pedagogy, teachers must engage in the kinds of sensitive discussions and careful study of MI theory that occurred in the schools described in this chapter. Without such a process, schools can adopt the trappings of MI without being true to its spirit; in short, MI becomes the end in itself, rather than the means of attaining an educational goal.

Using MI More as a Means than an End

In these well-intentioned but misguided efforts, MI becomes a list of categories to cover: a teacher's main concern is to ensure that all intelligences are experienced by all children, whether or not activities relate to the curriculum. MI becomes a new orthodoxy: children are labeled "linguistic" or "bodily-kinesthetic," disregarding the notion of intelligence as multifaceted and dynamic. Some schools work through this in the first stages of implementation, then become comfortable enough with MI to use it to help children master the curriculum by building on their individual strengths.

Teacher Collaboration

Collaboration and support systems are necessary if the approach is to become a major organizing principle in the school. Teamwork or collaboration is not unique to Spectrum-driven reform. What is distinctive, however, is how naturally collaborative relationships seem to develop, arising from needs specific to the approach. To integrate fully multiple intelligences and multiple disciplines into the curriculum, teachers often must call upon the domain expertise of other staff members. Working with art and music specialists, for example, can be particularly valuable as teachers try to incorporate the arts into projects and other aspects of the curriculum. Some schools use team teaching, pairing educators with different areas of expertise. Moreover, teachers need one another to provide friendly criticism and share ideas about curriculum activities, observational strategies, and reporting methods. Extending the definition a bit further, collaboration can include inviting parents into the classroom, working with other community members, and consulting experts in the field.

Through the process of collaboration, teachers not only develop a deeper understanding of the intelligences, but also gain valuable insights into one another. Teachers learn to capitalize on one another's areas of strength, using that knowledge for curriculum development and team-teaching. Collaboration also provides emotional and psychological support. For example, when trying to introduce new disciplines or skills into the classroom, teachers often need support for taking the risk or seeking advice in their own areas of weakness. As described in the portrait of Gloucester's Fuller School, regular meetings can offer teachers a safe environment for sharing experiences and discussing techniques that both achieved and fell short of their expectations.

Implementing Changes That Fit School Culture

In order for MI/Spectrum to work, the approach must be "homegrown." Skeptics are most likely to be converted into enthusiasts if they can see the relevance of the MI/Spectrum approach to their own lives. To fit the theory to a school's culture, faculty must first analyze the resources upon which they can build, identify the changes they are ready to make, and decide what educational goals they would like to achieve. On the basis of such self-study, sites can select the most appropriate content and direction, and modify the approach to best fit school needs.

In some cases, as demonstrated by Bruce Campbell, even a single individual can make radical changes in his or her classroom. But schoolwide change requires more than the hard work and enthusiasm of a few committed individuals, and is unlikely to take hold or last if imposed from "outside" or "above." The approach seems to work best in schools where many or all faculty members are invited into the process of applying the philosophical approach to the practicalities of their particular community. Schools that traditionally have invited teachers into the decision-making process—or that already recognize children's individual differences in their pedagogy—thus may find it easier to implement the MI/Spectrum approach.

In addition, teachers should implement changes at a rate that they find comfortable. In many cases, practitioners must take small steps as they embark on their journey. A school may start with a small pilot program, or encourage teachers to experiment with different formats in different rooms. For example, some teachers may start using Spectrum learning activities to introduce new domains to all their students, whereas other teachers may begin administering Spectrum assessments with a small number of children to answer specific questions about their strengths and interests. The small-step strategy allows teachers to see for themselves which procedures and ideas work best and should be implemented on a wider scale.

CONCLUDING NOTE

Preliminary findings from an investigation of effective applications of MI theory, which Project Zero undertook with support from the Geraldine R. Dodge Foundation and the Charles and Helen Schwab Foundation, suggest several markers in addition to the ones mentioned above. We call these practices "compass points" because they are not strict rules, but routes that others have found helpful in attaining their goals. One compass point is a commitment to the arts as an essential element of school life and a form of expression through which all children can share their ideas, no matter what language they speak or where their strengths lie. Another, demonstrated by the project approach at Briarcliff and other schools discussed in this chapter, is the commitment to giving students meaningful choices in the way in which they learn material and demonstrate their knowledge. A third is using MI to foster high-quality work—through such practices as engagement, emphasis on skill development, feedback, and reflection—across the entire student population. Often, schools that begin by using MI with a special group such as gifted or at-risk children later expand the program to improve the learning of all children. Overall, these findings show that MI and Spectrum can be implemented effectively in many different ways.

Change cannot be expected to occur overnight. School reforms will not be successful unless time is set aside for educators to talk with one another, pilot ideas, implement them, make mistakes, and learn from those mistakes. Extending the conversations to the greater school community, including students, parents, and civic leaders, can generate further support for change.

As more and more schools gain experience in putting Spectrum/MI theory into practice, we hope that the dialogue will burst the confines of school walls and expand across buildings, across districts, across states. Professional journals and conferences long have provided an opportunity for the sharing of ideas. New technology, such as the Internet, may make this kind of communication easier and more immediate, enabling educators at schools hundreds or thousands of miles apart to ask questions about and comment on one another's work. We look forward to learning many more lessons from "the field" as educators carry on the challenging enterprise of school reform.

NOTE

1. The percentage of African American and Hispanic students, who were among the populations targeted by the Javits grant, did not change during the model gifted and talented program (Kornhaber, 1997). This may be because of a "ceiling effect"; Montgomery Knolls already was participating in a countywide program, called Program of Assessment, Diagnosis, and Instruction, that placed potentially gifted minority children in self-contained classrooms that emphasized the use of critical-thinking strategies and offered integrated, hands-on, cooperative learning experiences.

REFERENCES

Campbell, B. (1992, Summer). Multiple intelligences in action. *Childhood Education*, 197–202.

Campbell, L., Campbell, B., & Dickinson, D. (1996). *Teaching and learning through multiple intelligences.* Needham Heights, MA: Allyn & Bacon.

Fuller School. (1995a). *Blackburn Project: A short description of Fuller MI program.* Gloucester, MA: Author.

Fuller School. (1995b). *Parent survey analysis.* Gloucester, MA: Author.

Fuller School. (1996). *MI notes: A publication of the Gloucester public schools' multiple intelligences program,* 3(7). Gloucester, MA: Author.

Gardner, H. (in press). Multiple approaches to understanding. In C. Reigeluth (Ed.), *Instructional-Design theories and models: Vol. 2.* Mahwah, NJ: Lawrence Erlbaum.

Harvard Project Zero. (1995). *People/schools that are interested in MI theory.* Cambridge, MA: Author.

Katz, L., & Chard, S. (1989). *Engaging children's minds: The project approach.* Norwood, NJ: Ablex.

Kornhaber, M. (1997). *Equitable identification for gifted education and the theory of multiple intelligences.* Unpublished doctoral dissertation. Harvard University, Cambridge, MA.

Krechevsky, M., & Seidel, S. (1998). Minds at work: Applying multiple intelligences in the classroom. In R. J. Sternberg & W. Williams (Eds.), *Intelligence, instruction, and assessment.* Hillsdale, NJ: Lawrence Erlbaum.

Parker, C. (1995, Fall). Multiple intelligences and Foxfire: A natural match. *Hands on,* 12–17.

CHAPTER 7

THE BRIDGES OF SPECTRUM

Howard Gardner

In the preceding pages, my colleagues and I have drawn you into our adventure: a journey of more than 10 years' duration, in which we have sought to develop a new approach to early childhood education. In truth, when we began the journey, we could anticipate neither the course nor the ultimate destination. We thought that we would develop a means of assessing talents in young children, and that the task would take about 4 years to complete. Instead, we discovered that assessment, curriculum, and pedagogy are inextricably intertwined; that the contours of early childhood education differ markedly across settings; and that, in the end, we would have not so much a new means of assessment but rather an educational approach that could be adapted by many individuals and groups for a variety of educational ends. Not that we have reached the end, of course; indeed, the vitality of Spectrum is best conveyed in the fact that its key ideas continue to be extended in new and unexpected directions.

BUILDING BRIDGES

As I reflect upon the course of Spectrum, I am struck by the extent to which we have had to navigate between opposing forces: the attraction of theory versus the realities of practice; the core ideas of Spectrum versus the goals and needs of various communities; a focus on the child as an individual versus a primary concern with a collectivity of children in a community. Sometimes we have been pulled too far in opposite directions and this has produced feelings of frustration; but on happier occasions, we have been able to construct a bridge that actually links these contrasting emphases. In these concluding notes I describe some of the ways in which these "bridges of Spectrum" have been constructed.

From Theory to Practice and Back Again

Like many researchers, we began our work with a relatively firm rooting in our own theories—in the present case, David Feldman's theory of development in domains, my ideas about multiple intelligences, and a general Piagetian slant toward human growth. In the early 1980s, we would have described our endeavor simply as an attempt to put the theory into practice.

Once we had begun to work in the classrooms of the Eliot-Pearson Children's School, however, it became clear that we had a great deal to learn about the lives that are led by young children, the routines of busy and effective teachers, and the agendas of the family and the community. If we were to be effective at all, we had to learn to watch and listen to those with whom we had formed a partnership. Again, at first, we might have thought that this was simply an issue of politeness or, more cynically, manipulation; however, we came to see that we had at least as much to learn from practitioners as vice versa.

Consider, for example, our belief that we could design tasks or games in isolation and bring them from the "lab" to the "field." Nothing could be further from the truth. Our most effective Spectrum tasks came from observations of what the children were already doing, what they liked to do, and the nature of their interactions with one another and with the teachers. Often, the simplest household materials or interactive games worked the best—glitz is in the eye of the often pint-sized beholder.

Or consider our initial focus on tasks that tapped the intelligences. Not only did we discover that there was no ready mapping from intelligence to domain; we soon learned that the ways in which children approached tasks could be as revealing as the particular content of a task. The initial list of seven intelligences grew sporadically until it reached 15 separate tasks in domains. We soon complemented our list of Spectrum tasks with a set of measures of "working styles." And this extension of our repertoire ended up yielding a point of considerable interest to developmental science. Rather than extending across the board, as the term *style* implies, working styles are sometimes quite content specific; a child may be impulsive or humorous with one set of materials, and reflective or sober with others. A full inventory of a child's proclivities must monitor *both* the contents with which the child is occupied and the approaches to that particular set of contents.

One of our areas of investigation yielded a much fuller delineation of a particular intelligence: instead of simply looking at interpersonal intelligence, we now distinguish roles such as leader, facilitator, team player, independent player, and caregiver/friend. And another area of Spectrum, the so-called naturalist's corner has actually led to the expounding of a new intelligence—that of the naturalist (Gardner, 1998).

We are by no means the only educationally oriented researchers to learn this lesson. Indeed, one of the most productive developments of the past decade has been the extent to which researchers and practitioners concerned with education have worked together, the extent to which practice has contributed substantively to research, and the ways in which theory has been strengthened through attention to effective practice (McGilly, 1994). Beyond question, these bridges have strengthened both sides of the enterprise.

Spectrum Needs Versus Community Needs

Even as our own ideas were enriched by our daily interactions with practitioners, we were as often reminded that the needs and goals of the research team were by no means identical to those of the communities in which we were working.

This tension was partially masked at the Eliot-Pearson Children's School. This "lab school" has for many years been affiliated with a major research center in child development, and ready and easy intercourse obtains between the two institutions. Many of the individuals involved in the project were students or graduates of the research program, and prestige in the school was at least loosely linked to research credentials.

Once we began to work in other communities, whether in public schools or in museum settings, the different goals and orientations of the participating institutions stood out in increasingly sharp relief. Researchers are driven by theories that they want to test and questions that they want to answer; they evaluate their success by the extent to which they can progress on these two fronts. Prestige inheres in the capacity to give talks or to write papers (or even three books!) that chronicle what has been discovered. As a wag once cynically observed:

> The researcher who researches and runs away,
> Lives to research another day.

Schools and museums have entirely different agendas and priorities. Supported by taxpayer money (and private donations) rather than by research funds, they are expected to educate, to entertain, or both. Teachers and curators carry heavy administrative and organizational burdens. They have legal obligations to the children, and equally ponderous moral obligations to their community. Their success is evaluated by relatively objective measures (test scores, attendance, box office receipts) and, more subjectively, by the general approval or disapproval of the relevant communities. Although they may agree to participate in research out of feelings of good citizenship, or with the hope that they may benefit from an association with a prestigious university, the questions that drive the researchers—and even the answers that are secured—are rarely pressing ones for those who are daily charged with educating young children.

We encountered many concrete instances of these differing agendas. At the Eliot-Pearson Children's School, we wanted to see children in isolation; yet the school placed a premium on children working together in groups. We wanted to focus in our reports on the strengths of children, but parents wanted to know about the children's areas of weakness. Working with the school-and-museum collaboration, we sought to develop materials that "resonated" in the various settings; yet the relatively controlled environment of the classroom is quite different from the avowed "free choice" of the museum setting—and parents of children could not readily grasp the utility of the "home materials" that we developed. When working in first-grade classrooms, we emphasized the importance of different interests, styles, and paces at the very time that teachers were feeling pressured to teach reading and to secure high test scores for their often disadvantaged populations.

Faced with these different priorities, one human impulse is to search for compromise—to try to find materials or approaches or goals that serve both constituencies. Sometimes, this is easy to do—for example, there was no problem in providing parents with a wider range of information about their children's intellectual profiles.

However, compromise is not always possible or advisable. A more effective bridge, I suggest, can be built when individuals come to know one another well and develop a sense of trust; and when they affirm that they do share certain common goals, for example, better serving the variety of young children in their care today. Under such circumstances, the parties can comfortably accept that they have different agendas and understand that each party respects and honors the agenda of the other. And so, for example, the school (and its personnel) can work effectively with the museum (and its personnel) if both parties recognize the legitimate goals and priorities of the other party; and if they acknowledge, equally, that children are better served if both the school and the museum have the opportunity to impact the child in a positive way. Or the researchers can honor the parents' primary interest in the well-roundedness of the children, while the parents respect the researchers' desire to figure out what educational approaches are most likely to work for a variety of children.

Focus on the Child Versus Focus on Children

So long as we speak only to our colleagues, we psychologists are confirmed in our belief that the world consists primarily of the space between the two ears—the mind/brain. Developmental psychology is particularly guilty of this sin, since our own patron saint Jean Piaget was interested precisely in the characteristics of the Mind that are shared by all children—and not particularly interested in interactions among children or in the place of the child in the wider community. Our own work recognizes the dynamic interactions among children and yet it too has had as its primary thrust a concentration on what is special about each child's mind.

Making this case in the United States is less difficult than making it in other societies, because our society focuses significantly on the individual child. Yet a classroom is not simply a collection of isolated atoms; it is a community of persons and it can only work if individuals know one another, respect one another, and adhere to various consensual norms. Moreover, recent research and experimentation indicates that a focus on the individual qua individual does not do a service to many children in our society: children often perform better when they have been learning in well-designed groups; and effective functioning in adult society depends significantly upon a capacity to become an effective member of a team and to have one's own strengths and weaknesses complemented by those of other individuals.

In the theory undergirding Spectrum, there is certainly recognition of the role of other individuals. David Feldman acknowledges the importance of the community in nurturing talents, and my own work stresses the centrality of the personal intelligences. Still, it can be said that our focus remains largely on the individual child, whereas from the point of view of the institutions with which we worked, the health of the wider community has been a priority—and properly so.

When it comes to constructing bridges in this area, we developed a few promising approaches. In the Project Spectrum first-grade class, for example, learning centers were places in which children could work together in areas of mutual interest, using their intellectual strengths in a synergistic way. In the collaboration among school, museum, and home, the concept of resonance was another tool for linking the individual child with persons and resources that were generally available. Our mentor program highlighted the special role that a caring adult from the community can play in the mind of a young child.

Perhaps most important, however, was a bridge that was conceptual rather than material. At its most successful, the Spectrum approach helps those with a focus on the individual realize that development cannot take place without a marshaling of "distributed" human and artifactual resources; and it helps those with a focus on the community to appreciate how each individual can make an idiosyncratic yet important contribution to the wider community. After administering Spectrum tasks to several youngsters, one of our most gifted teachers said, "I have never known so much about the individual children in my class." This teacher was able to use this knowledge in order to construct a more effective community, thereby productively bridging the often isolated entities of child and milieu.

SPECTRUM WARNING SIGNS

For the most part, we have been delighted by the extent to which other individuals, often in quite remote settings, have found Spectrum ideas and practices to be generative in their own work. As indicated in Chapter 6, we have learned a great deal from observing the often ingenious implementations undertaken by these colleagues.

Occasionally, however, we encounter applications that seem to go against the spirit of Spectrum. We should perhaps assume part of the blame for some of these flawed practices, because we earlier were privy to some misapprehensions ourselves. For example, our initial thoughts were much closer to the idea of developing a battery of seven or so "quick and dirty" tests, and when Spectrum is used in this psychometric way, our cringing has a twinge of guilt attached to it.

Generally speaking, we think of Spectrum as a promising way of discovering a great deal about youngsters at a particular historical moment in their lives. However, we are leery of assuming that a child can be described at any age as "linguistic but not spatial" or as "likely to become a naturalist but incapable of becoming a mechanic." Our measures are too rough, our understanding of human development way too uncertain, to allow such kinds of capsule statements. Also, there are virtually no longitudinal data to suggest the extent to which a profile that is valid at one age will necessarily endure 2 years, let alone 2 decades.

Indeed, our belief as developmentalists is that human growth is always a result in part of cultural interventions and in part of individual will. Whether the "child naturalist" can become an "adolescent mechanic" reflects what the child wants to do and is willing to invest time in doing, and how well structured the training and opportunities are in his or her milieu.

It is also important to underscore, once again, that an intelligence is not equivalent to a domain, discipline, or task. We may speak as if it is possible to identify the operating intelligences in a child, but that is simply a convenient shorthand, at most. "Intelligences" are a scientific construct, not a physical reality. In fact, all we can ever look at, as psychologists and educators, are the kinds of tasks, skills, and domains that the child can master. And so it is much more prudent to say that Child A is a novice guitar player but is already at a journeyman level in identifying plants and animals, than it is to invoke a putatively scientific characterization of the child as "musically" or "naturalistically" intelligent.

Finally, in the light of our earlier discussion, it is important to recognize that Spectrum needs to serve different masters, each with its own agenda. We suggest that the bridges that we have identified can be useful to most individuals who become involved with Spectrum. Accordingly, we encourage future collaborators to recognize, but to avoid becoming ensnared in, the tensions between theory and practice; the conflicts between Spectrum agendas and those of cooperating institutions; and the contrasting pulls of a focus on the individual and a focus on the wider community. Perhaps some of our own bridges can be suggestive in this regard; we will continue to learn from others who are implementing Spectrum-inspired approaches.

FUTURE LINES

No doubt Alfred Binet would be astonished to find what has happened to his ideas—and his test items—in the 90-odd years since he first began to examine Parisian schoolchildren. Even in the 10 years of our own work, we have been continually surprised by the directions that we ourselves have taken (perhaps, more properly, the directions in which our work has propelled us): and we have been equally astonished by the often inspired applications devised by individuals whom we only know casually or indeed have never even met at all.

Spectrum is not a package, not a cookbook— as we have sometimes quipped, "We don't have a kit, we don't even have a caboodle." Perhaps that void is to the good in terms of both practice and longevity. Practices are most likely to make sense and most likely to last if they are home-grown, rather than imposed from outside. We expect that innovations will continue to occur and that the most important future of Spectrum lies in the hands—and the tasks and the learning centers—of caring educators.

As for our own research interests, we remain curious about the factors that lead to a particular configuration of gifts in the young child, and the factors that determine how those gifts will continue to unfold—or fail to unfold—in various kinds of environments. Indeed, to the extent that

Spectrum approaches are undertaken with different populations, different ages, and in different societies, the story of Spectrum will gain exciting chapters. We also recognize the need for adaptations of Spectrum that are targeted toward traditional psychometric concerns; given the enormous current pressures for accountability, even at the early childhood level, those who would champion Spectrum need to provide evidence of its reliability, validity, efficiency, and overall effectiveness.

It would not be easy to secure funds to carry out studies of these issues; lamentably, we live at a time when funds for basic research at the intersection of developmental and educational issues are almost nonexistent. However, even without separately funded research, it should be possible to determine the broad outline of answers to some of the questions that continue to animate our interest. And some day, a happier day, when a more enlightened funding climate arrives, it should become possible again to investigate questions about the education of our young children in a systematic way.

FINAL THANKS

Researchers are driven by curiosity and it is deceptive to claim that all research must have a ready (and anticipated) application. Yet it should be evident that much of good practice—though by no means all—comes out of careful research, pursued in a disinterested way over a significant period of time. We could never have undertaken Spectrum at all—and could certainly not have reached any conclusions—without the generous support of several foundations. To the extent that Spectrum has had an effect, and continues to have an effect, we are not alone in our indebtedness to the Rockefeller Brothers Fund, the W. T. Grant Foundation, and, above all, the Spencer Foundation.

Returning to the first person, in closing, David Feldman and I want to express our profound thanks to the many persons and institutions that made this work possible. We cannot enumerate everyone here; but we would be remiss if we did not single out for special thanks our colleagues at the Eliot-Pearson School, the Children's Museum of Boston, the Mason School in Boston, and the Winter Hill School of the city of Somerville, Massachusetts.

We are grateful as well to the hundreds of children, parents, teachers, docents, and mentors who participated in various ways. And as should be evident from the previous pages, we owe our largest debt to the wonderful cohort of researchers and practitioners who worked directly with us—

chief among them Mara Krechevsky, Julie Viens, and Jackie Chen—valiant researchers—and to Emily Isberg, who in the course of editing three disparate manuscripts, became an honorary member of the Spectrum team.

REFERENCES

Gardner, H. (1998). Are there additional intelligences? In J. Kane (Ed.), *Education, information, and transformation*. Englewood Cliffs, NJ: Prentice Hall.
McGilly, K. (Ed.). (1994) *Classroom lessons*. Cambridge, MA: MIT Press.

DESCRIPTION OF SPECTRUM ACTIVITIES

MOVEMENT ACTIVITIES

Creative Movement: Children participate in creative movement sessions every 2 weeks throughout the school year. This ongoing curriculum focuses on children's abilities in five areas of dance and creative movement: sensitivity to rhythm, expressiveness, body control, generation of movement ideas, and responsiveness to music. Teachers use a balance of semistructured activities (such as Simon Says) and more open-ended activities (such as interpretive dancing to music).

Obstacle Course: In the spring, an outdoor obstacle course provides children with the opportunity to participate in sequences involving complex and combined movements. The course includes a long jump, a balance beam, an obstacle run, and a hurdle jump. These stations draw upon skills found in many different sports, such as coordination, timing, balance, and power.

LANGUAGE ACTIVITIES

Storyboard Activity: The Storyboard Activity is designed to provide a concrete but open-ended framework in which a child can create stories. Children are asked to tell a story using a storyboard equipped with an ambiguous-looking landscape, foliage, dwellings, and assorted figures, creatures, and props (e.g., king, dragon, and jewel box). The activity measures a range of language skills including complexity of vocabulary and sentence structure, use of narrative voice and dialogue, thematic coherence, and expressiveness.

Adapted from M. Krechevsky. (1998). *Project Spectrum: Preschool Assessment Handbook.* Project Zero Frameworks for Early Childhood Education, Vol. 3. New York: Teachers College Press.

Reporter Activities: The Reporter Activities assess a child's ability to describe an event he or she has experienced. In the first activity, the child watches a movie and then is asked a series of questions about it. His or her answers are scored in terms of accuracy of content, complexity of vocabulary, level of detail, and sentence structure. Weekend News assesses similar skills, but is conducted throughout the year. Every week or 2, children pretend to be reporters and tell what they did over the weekend. Their accounts, which are frequently a combination of real-world and fantasy events, are recorded by an adult and collected in a special notebook. The notebook provides multiple samples of a child's reporting skills that can be reviewed through the year.

MATHEMATICS ACTIVITIES

Dinosaur Game: The Dinosaur Game is designed to measure the child's counting skills, understanding of number concepts, ability to adhere to rules, and use of strategy. The game consists of a game board with a picture of a large dinosaur, wooden dice, and small plastic dinosaurs for game pieces. The object of the game is for the small dinosaurs to escape from the hungry mouth of the large dinosaur. Two players take turns throwing dice to determine the direction and the number of spaces they each can move. At the end of the game, the child is permitted to arrange the dice to his or her own best advantage, revealing how well he or she understands the rules.

Bus Game: The purpose of the Bus Game is to assess the child's ability to create a useful notation system, perform mental calculations, and organize number information with one or more variables. The Bus Game consists of a cardboard bus, a game board with four bus stops, figures that get on and off the bus, and two sets of colored chips. In the game, the child is asked to keep track of how many people are riding the bus as it makes a number of stops. Each trip becomes increasingly challenging. For some trips the child uses colored chips to keep count of the passengers; for other trips the child is asked to keep count in his or her head.

SCIENCE ACTIVITIES

Discovery Area: The Discovery Area is a year-round area of the classroom devoted to natural science activities. Activities include caring for small animals, growing plants, and examining a range of natural materials such as rocks and shells. Although the Discovery activities are not formally scored, teachers use a checklist to record information about children's observations and their appreciation and understanding of natural phenomena. For example, some children notice similarities and dissimilarities between materials as well as changes over time; others ask questions based on their observations in order to find out more about an item in the area.

Treasure Hunt Game: The Treasure Hunt Game is designed to assess the child's ability to make logical inferences. Before the game starts, different types of "treasure" are hidden under a number of different flags. The object of the game is for the child to figure out the rule governing the placement of the treasures, and use this rule to predict where he or she will find particular types of objects. The child is given a color-coded box to use to keep track of the treasures that he or she finds, but is not instructed how to use it. The way that the child uses the box to sort the treasures can reflect how well he or she organizes information and can also help the child figure out the rule.

Sink and Float Activity: The Sink and Float Activity is used to assess a child's ability to generate hypotheses based on his or her observations and to conduct simple experiments. The child is shown a tub of water and an assortment of floating and sinking materials. Then, he or she is asked to make a series of predictions about the objects and to generate a hypothesis to explain their behavior. The child is encouraged also to try out his or her own ideas for experimenting with the materials.

Assembly Activity: The Assembly Activity is designed to measure the child's mechanical ability. The child is presented with two food grinders to take apart and put back together. Successful completion of the activity depends on fine motor skills and visual-spatial abilities as well as a range of observational and problem-solving abilities. This activity, in particular, reveals important cognitive skills that might be overlooked in more traditional programs.

SOCIAL ACTIVITIES

Classroom Model: The purpose of the Classroom Model is to assess the child's ability to observe and analyze social events and experiences in the classroom. The child is presented with a small replica of the classroom, complete with furnishings and wooden figures with photographs of classmates and teachers attached. In much the same way as in playing with a dollhouse, the child can arrange the figures in the classroom model to reflect his or her understanding of peers, teachers, and social experiences. The child is asked questions about his or her own preferences for activities and friendships as well as the preferences and friendships of classmates. Awareness of social roles (e.g., which children act as leaders or facilitators) is probed as well.

Peer Interaction Checklist: Teachers use a checklist to help them observe closely and assess the way in which children interact with peers. After completing the checklist, teachers determine whether a child consistently assumes any of four distinctive social roles: leader, facilitator, independent player, or team player. Each role is associated with specific types of behavior; for example, a child identified as a facilitator often enjoys sharing information with or helping other children; a child who assumes the role of leader often attempts to organize other children.

VISUAL ARTS ACTIVITIES

Art Portfolios: Throughout the school year, each child's artwork is collected in a portfolio. These portfolios include drawings, paintings, collages, and three-dimensional pieces. Twice a year, teachers can review and assess the contents according to criteria that include the child's use of lines and shapes, color, space, detail, and representation and design. The child's preferred medium is noted also.

Structured Activities: In addition to the portfolios, four structured art activities are introduced to the class each year and assessed on criteria similar to those used in the portfolio assessment. Children are asked to complete three drawings and one three-dimensional task. These activities give every child in the group the chance to respond to the same assignment and interact with the same materials.

MUSIC ACTIVITIES

Singing Activity: The Singing Activity is designed to assess the child's ability to maintain accurate pitch and rhythm while singing, and the ability to recall a song's musical properties. During the activity, the child is asked to sing his or her favorite song and a popular children's song. The child is also asked to recall a song taught to the class prior to the activity.

Music Perception Activity: The purpose of the Music Perception Activity is to assess a child's ability to discriminate pitch in different situations. In the first part of the activity, the first four phrases of three familiar tunes are played on a tape recorder and the child is asked to identify the tunes as soon as he or she recognizes them. During the next part of the task, the child listens to different versions of a familiar tune and is asked to identify which are correct and which are incorrect. In the last components of the activity, the child plays two pitch-matching games using Montessori bells, which look identical but produce different tones.

WORKING STYLES

Working Styles Checklist: The Working Styles Checklist helps teachers examine the ways in which a child approaches materials and tasks. Teachers fill out the checklist for each child after he or she completes each Spectrum activity. Examples of working styles include persistent, playful, focused, reluctant to engage, and eager to transform the task to suit personal interests. The checklist helps teachers identify whether there are particular domains or types of situations in which the child works most effectively. For example, the child may be focused when working on assembly or visual arts projects, but easily distracted in other domains; or, the child may be confident when performing highly structured tasks, but hesitant when asked to make up a story.

PROJECT SPECTRUM KEY ABILITIES

Mechanics and Construction

Understanding of Causal and Functional Relationships

- infers relationships based on observation
- understands relationship of parts to whole, the function of these parts, and how parts are put together

Visual-Spatial Abilities

- is able to construct or reconstruct physical objects and simple machines in two or three dimensions
- understands spatial relationships between parts of a mechanical object

Problem-Solving Approach With Mechanical Objects

- uses and learns from trial-and-error approach
- uses systematic approach in solving mechanical problems
- compares and generalizes information

Fine Motor Skills

- is adept at manipulating small parts or objects
- exhibits good hand-eye coordination (e.g., hammers on head of nail rather than on fingers)

Adapted from J. Q. Chen. (Ed.) (1998) *Project Spectrum: Early Learning Activities.* Project Zero Frameworks for Early Childhood Education, Vol. 2. New York: Teachers College Press.

Science

Observational Skills

- engages in close observation of materials to learn about their physical characteristics; uses one or more of the senses
- often notices changes in the environment (e.g., new leaves on plants, bugs on trees, subtle seasonal changes)
- shows interest in recording observations through drawings, charts, sequence cards, or other methods

Identification of Similarities and Differences

- likes to compare and contrast materials, events, or both
- classifies materials, notices similarities, differences, or both between specimens (e.g., compares and contrasts crabs and spiders)

Hypothesis Formation and Experimentation

- makes predictions based on observations
- asks "what if"-type questions and offers explanations for why things are the way they are
- conducts simple experiments or generates ideas for experiments to test own or others' hypotheses (e.g., drops large and small rocks in water to see if one size sinks faster than the other; waters plant with paint instead of water)

Interest in/Knowledge of Nature and Scientific Phenomena

- exhibits extensive knowledge about various scientific topics; spontaneously offers information about these topics or reports on own or others' experience with natural world
- shows interest in natural phenomena, or related materials such as natural history books, over extended periods of time
- regularly asks questions about things observed

Movement

Body Control

- shows an awareness of and ability to isolate and use different body parts
- plans, sequences, and executes moves efficiently—movements do not seem random or disjointed
- is able to replicate one's own movements and those of others

Sensitivity to Rhythm
- moves in synchrony with stable or changing rhythms, particularly in music (e.g., child attempts to move with the rhythm, as opposed to being unaware of or disregarding rhythmic changes)
- is able to set a rhythm of one's own and regulate it to achieve a desired effect

Expressiveness

- evokes moods and images through movement using gestures and body postures; stimulus can be a verbal image, a prop, or music
- is able to respond to mood or tonal quality of an instrument or music selection (e.g., uses light and fluid movements for lyrical music versus strong and staccato movements for a march)

Generation of Movement Ideas

- is able to invent interesting and novel movement ideas, verbally, physically, or both or offer extensions of ideas (e.g., suggesting that children raise their arms to look like clouds floating in the sky)
- responds immediately to ideas and images with original movements
- choreographs a simple dance, perhaps teaching it to others

Responsiveness to Music

- responds differently to different kinds of music
- shows sensitivity to rhythm and expressiveness when responding to music
- explores available space (vertical and horizontal) comfortably using different levels, moving easily and fluidly around the space
- anticipates others in a shared space
- experiments with moving own body in space (e.g., turning and spinning)

Music

Perception
- is sensitive to dynamics (loud and soft)
- is sensitive to tempo and rhythmic patterns
- discriminates pitch
- identifies musical and musicians' styles
- identifies different instruments and sounds

Production

- is able to maintain accurate pitch
- is able to maintain accurate tempo and rhythmic patterns
- exhibits expressiveness when singing or playing instrument
- can recall and reproduce musical properties of songs and other compositions

Composition

- creates simple compositions with some sense of beginning, middle, and end
- creates simple notation system

Math

Numerical Reasoning

- is adept at calculations (e.g., finds shortcuts)
- is able to estimate
- is adept at quantifying objects and information (e.g., by record keeping, creating effective notation, graphing)
- is able to identify numerical relationships (e.g., probability, ratio)

Spatial Reasoning

- finds spatial patterns
- is adept with puzzles
- uses imagery to visualize and conceptualize a problem

Logical Problem Solving

- focuses on relationships and overall structure of problem instead of isolated facts

- makes logical inferences
- generalizes rules
- develops and uses strategies (e.g., when playing games)

Social Understanding

Understanding of Self

- identifies own abilities, skills, interests, and areas of difficulty
- reflects upon own feelings, experiences, and accomplishments
- draws upon these reflections to understand and guide own behavior
- shows insight into the factors that cause an individual to do well or have difficulty in an area

Understanding of Others

- demonstrates knowledge of peers and their activities
- attends closely to others
- recognizes others' thoughts, feelings, and abilities
- draws conclusions about others based on their activities

Assumption of Distinctive Social Roles Leader

- often initiates and organizes activities
- organizes other children
- assigns roles to others
- explains how activity is carried out
- oversees and directs activities

Facilitator

- often shares ideas, information, and skills with other children
- mediates conflict
- invites other children to play
- extends and elaborates other children's ideas
- provides help when others need attention

Caregiver/Friend:

- comforts other children when they are upset
- shows sensitivity to other children's feelings
- shows understanding of friends' likes and dislikes

Language

Invented narrative/storytelling

- uses imagination and originality in storytelling
- enjoys listening to or reading stories
- exhibits interest and ability in plot design and development, character elaboration and motivation, descriptions of settings, scenes, or moods, use of dialogue, and so on
- shows performing ability or dramatic flair, including a distinctive style, expressiveness, or an ability to play a variety of roles

Descriptive language/reporting

- provides accurate and coherent accounts of events, feelings, and experiences (e.g., uses correct sequence and appropriate level of detail; distinguishes fact from fantasy)
- provides accurate labels and descriptions for things
- shows interest in explaining how things work, or describing a procedure
- engages in logical argument or inquiry

Poetic use of language/wordplay

- enjoys and is adept at wordplay such as puns, rhymes, metaphors
- plays with word meanings and sounds
- demonstrates interest in learning new words
- uses words in a humorous fashion

Visual Arts

Perception

- aware of visual elements in the environment and in artwork (e.g., color, lines, shapes, patterns, detail)
- sensitive to different artistic styles (e.g., can distinguish abstract art from realism, impressionism, etc.)

Production: Representation

- able to represent visual world accurately in two or three dimensions
- able to create recognizable symbols for common objects (e.g., people,

vegetation, houses, animals) and coordinate elements spatially into uni-
fied whole
- uses realistic proportions, detailed features, deliberate choice of color

Artistry

- able to use various elements of art (e.g., line, color, shape) to depict
emotions, produce certain effects, and embellish drawings or three-
dimensional work
- conveys strong mood through literal representation (e.g., smiling sun,
crying face) and abstract features (e.g., dark colors or drooping lines to
express sadness); produces drawings or sculptures that appear "lively,"
"sad," or "powerful"
- shows concern with decoration and embellishment
- produces drawings that are colorful, balanced, rhythmic, or a combination of these

Exploration

- flexible and inventive in use of art materials (e.g., experiments with
paint, chalk, clay)
- uses lines and shapes to generate a wide variety of forms (e.g., open and
closed, explosive and controlled) in two- or three-dimensional work
- able to execute a range of subjects or themes (e.g., people, animals,
buildings, landscapes)

ABOUT THE AUTHORS AND EDITORS

Jie-Qi Chen is Assistant Professor of Child Development and Early Education at the Erikson Institute in Chicago. She received a B.A. in education from Beijing Normal University, China and a Ph.D. in child development from Tufts University. She has worked as a researcher at Harvard Project Zero and as an instructor at Shannxi Teacher's College in China. Her research has focused on the development of domain-specific abilities in young children, alternative assessment, school reform, and cultural variation in child development. Her contributions have been included in D. P. Flanagan, J. L. Genshaft, and P. L. Harrison (Eds.), *Beyond traditional intellectual assessment: Contemporary and emerging theories, tests, and issues,* and the journal *International Education.*

David Henry Feldman is Professor in the Eliot-Pearson Department of Child Development at Tufts University, where he has served since 1974. He holds degrees from the University of Rochester, Harvard, and Stanford, where he was awarded the Ph.D. in 1969. His research interests involve developmental theory, studies of transitions and transformations in cognitive development, extremes in intellectual development, and creativity. His books include *Beyond Universals in Cognitive Development; Nature's Gambit: Child Prodigies and the Development of Human Potential* (with Lynn T. Goldsmith); and *Changing the World: A Framework for the Study of Creativity* (with Mihaly Czikszentmihalyi and Howard Gardner).

Howard Gardner is the John H. and Elisabeth A. Hobbs Professor of Cognition and Education and Adjunct Professor of Psychology at Harvard University, Adjunct Professor of Neurology at the Boston University School of Medicine, and Co-Director of Harvard Project Zero. He was awarded a MacArthur Prize Fellowship in 1981 and in 1990 he received the University of Louisville's Grawemeyer Award in Education for his theory of multiple intelligences. Most recently, he has conducted intensive case studies of exemplary creators and leaders, exploring the relationship between cutting-edge work in different domains and a sense of social responsibility. He is the author of 18 books, including *Frames of Mind; Art, Mind, and Brain;* and *Extraordinary Minds.*

Emily Isberg is a freelance writer and editor. She holds a B.A. from Harvard University and an M.S. from Columbia Graduate School of Journalism. She has worked as an assistant press secretary in the U.S. Senate, a reporter for the *Montgomery County Sentinel,* a science reporter for the *Harvard University Gazette,* and has taught classes at the toddler through high school level. Her articles have been published in *The Washington Post, Harvard Magazine,* and *Boston Magazine.* She is the author of the children's book *Peak Performance: Sports, Science, and the Body in Action.*

Mara Krechevsky has worked as an educational researcher at Harvard Project Zero for 15 years and holds a B.A. in philosophy and psychology from Yale University. From 1987 to 1992, she served as director of Project Spectrum, a research project implementing multiple intelligences theory in early childhood. She has consulted with schools across the country, written numerous articles (and book chapters, many co-authored with Howard Gardner), and given presentations on multiple intelligences theory and its educational implications, both in the U.S. and abroad. She currently directs a cross-cultural collaboration involving Harvard Project Zero and the municipal preschools and infant-toddler centers of Reggio Emilia, Italy, that is designed to create methods of documenting and assessing group learning. Krechevsky is the author of *Project Spectrum: Preschool Assessment Handbook.*

Julie Viens has worked as a researcher at Harvard Project Zero for 10 years, investigating the educational application of multiple intelligences theory. Viens, who earned a Ed.M. at Harvard University and a B.A. at New College (Sarasota, Florida), has a special interest in applying MI theory with ESL and disadvantaged populations. She currently co-directs the Adult Multiple Intelligences Project, part of the federally-funded National Center for the Study of Adult Learning and Literacy at Harvard University. She is a co-author of *Pathways to Multiple Intelligences: A Professional Development Guide,* (with B. Slatin and S. Baum in consultation with Howard Gardner), to be published by the American Psychological Association.

INDEX